INDIA ON TRIAL

INDIA ON TRIAL

A STUDY OF PRESENT CONDITIONS

J. E. WOOLACOTT

GYAN

Published by

Gyan Publishing House
5, Ansari Road
Daryaganj, New Delhi-110002
Phone: 011-47034999, 9811692060
E-mail: books@gyanbooks.com

Distribution Network
gyanbooks.com
India, USA, Canada, UK, Australia

ISBN: 978-93-7447-032-9 (PB)

First Published, 1929

2nd Impression 2026

Printed at: Gyan Press, Delhi.

INDIA ON TRIAL
Author: J. E. WOOLACOTT

INDIA ON TRIAL

INDIA ON TRIAL

A STUDY OF PRESENT CONDITIONS

BY

J. E. WOOLACOTT

FORMERLY CORRESPONDENT OF 'THE TIMES' AT DELHI AND SIMLA

'IN CONDITIONS MORE FAVOURABLE TO COOL JUDGMENT, I SUPPOSE THAT MOST PERSONS WOULD ADMIT THAT BRITISH INDIA AS WE FIND IT TODAY IS A BRITISH CREATION, AND THAT IT IS BRITISH POWER WHICH HAS DURING THE LAST CENTURY HELD TOGETHER ITS CONSTITUENT PARTS. IF THIS CENTRIPETAL INFLUENCE IS IMMEDIATELY OR TOO SUDDENLY WITHDRAWN, IS IT WHOLLY UNREASONABLE TO FEAR THAT SOME, AT ANY RATE, OF THE PARTS MIGHT FLY ASUNDER, AND THE DREAM OF A STRONG UNITED INDIA, A NATION AMONG THE NATIONS OF THE WORLD, AS WE MAY SPEAK OF THE BRITISH OR AMERICAN NATIONS, WOULD VANISH AND BE DESTROYED?'

LORD IRWIN, VICEROY OF INDIA, IN AN ADDRESS TO THE INDIAN LEGISLATIVE ASSEMBLY, ON 28TH JANUARY, 1929

MACMILLAN AND CO., LIMITED
ST. MARTIN'S STREET, LONDON
1929

CONTENTS

FOREWORD

The importance of India to the British Empire is vaguely recognised by many who have no real conception of the problems of that vast country. The responsibility of the British as trustees for the Indian people is also admitted in a general way. It is further realised, at all events by merchants, manufacturers and bankers, that India constitutes the greatest market in the world for British goods, and that the employment of large numbers of British industrial workers is dependent on the maintenance of our commerce with that country. A sense of communal obligation and of enlightened self-interest alike should, therefore, impel every thoughtful citizen to acquaint himself with the achievements of the British in India, the situation which exists in India to-day and the gravity of the Indian problems that await solution. The need for enlightenment is all the more insistent in that within the past few years a number of British politicians possessing a superficial knowledge of Indian affairs have sought to create the impression that our administration is characterised by callous oppression and is perpetuating a system which inflicts poverty and misery on the masses of the people. How far assertions of this nature gain credence it is impossible to say. But the atmosphere created by the incessant repetition of the fallacious teachings of pseudo-historians regarding the actions of British administrators in the past and the misrepresentation o. British policy in the present constitutes a menace alike to Great Britain and to India which it would be folly to ignore. In India itself, especially among the rising generation, the most grotesque fallacies are avidly accepted. It has been my good fortune on a number of occasions to be invited to take part in the discussions of University students in India, and it came as a revelation to me to discover how thoroughly the minds of many young men had been permeated by the doctrines of anti-British propagandists, who, in season and out of season, assert that our rule in India has impoverished the people, and that measures enacted for the protection of law-abiding Indians against the forces of disorder have been inspired by a determination to fix the yoke of slavery more firmly on the neck of India. These misconceptions seemed in the main to be based on honest conviction, and it was of good omen that the students listened with courtesy and obvious interest to a frank exposition of the other side of the question.

Unfortunately for India, sound and sober Indian opinion seldom finds vocal expression.

Emboldened, therefore, by the effect created upon uninformed minds and cherishing the fallacious hope that their impassioned words may cause consternation in this country, Swarajist leaders are declaring their goal to be an independent India. One of the most prominent of these gentlemen, a well-known Bengali politician, in his presidential address to a conference at Poona, recently described the means by which this end was to be achieved. Non-co-operation and boycott on a national scale, would, he said, be possible when the national will was roused. The movement would reach its climax in a general strike or *hartal* coupled with a boycott of British goods, and there would be some form of civil disobedience. There would thus be a paralysis of administration and possibly of foreign trade and commerce. The bureaucracy would then be forced to yield to the demands of "the people's representatives."

The doctrine thus expounded has been preached from many platforms, and it has been made apparent that the industrial classes are regarded by extremist politicians as mere pawns in a sordid and ignoble game. Soviet Russia watches this development with malicious satisfaction, and though hitherto Bolshevist intrigue has failed of its main purpose in India, the danger of civil commotion with all its terrible concomitants is ever present.

The great work of reconstruction carried on under British administration has been impeded in recent years by mischievous and dangerous agitations, and to-day reckless men, who have been justly described by the Viceroy, Lord Irwin, as "false friends" of India, are clamouring for the severance of the British connexion.

What would happen, asked a distinguished Punjabi soldier, Colonel Sir Umar Hyat Khan, in the Council of State, if the British were to leave India? "The Punjab," he said, "would take as large a portion of the country as is near it; Nepal would take another part, and the Ruling Chiefs would take all the territory round them, and so on, until perhaps our friends from the Frontier would come down upon us and sweep us, or perhaps another Eastern nation might attack our seaports." Can it be imagined that the truth of this word picture is not realised by the political orators who expatiate on the necessity of expelling the British? In the hour of danger the value of the British soldier has again and again been publicly acknowledged. In 1919, when an attempted invasion of India by Afghanistan led to the death of many brave British and Indian soldiers in the grim regions of the North-West Frontier, a Bengali journal which is an inveterate and vehement critic of the existing regime in India, almost hysterically called for a cessation of political agitation and for united support for the Government lest the success of the fierce invaders from the North should bring trouble into the lives of Indians yet unborn.

While, then, the idea of driving the British out of India by force is an idle phantasy, there is grave danger to that country in the agitations set on foot by reckless politicians, who after inflaming the passions of the masses by mendacious propaganda, have not the power, even if they have the inclination, to check the excesses committed by their dupes. The injury inflicted upon the people of India by agitation in the past ten years is incalculable. From the North-West Frontier to Malabar in the far south, and from the Bombay Presidency to Assam there have been witnessed scenes of disorder and bloodshed, often accompanied by barbarous atrocities, to say nothing of widespread destruction of property. No Constitutional reforms within the bounds of reason will satisfy the men whose utterances have been instrumental in causing outbreaks of violence. Their interest in the economic condition of the masses is usually perfunctory and incidental to the agitation of the moment. It may be hoped, therefore, that the policy of attempting to placate the implacable which has too often been prominent in high places has now been definitely abandoned.

In considering the future of India, the natural and laudable desire of responsible Indians to have an increasing share in the government of their country has to be kept actively in mind. It has equally to be remembered that Western conceptions of government have not the appeal to Oriental peoples that we are prone to believe. That truth has found repeated expression of late and it is likely to be impressed on Sir John Simon and his colleagues. That a strong central Government must be maintained in order to facilitate stability and progress in India is beyond all doubt. The position of the Indian States, whose Princes rule over 72,000,000 subjects, will also have to receive fuller recognition than has been accorded to it in the past.

The task entrusted to the Simon Commission has been described by Lord Birkenhead as a momentous one, and, in view of the vast issues involved, it is essential, in the interests both of the Indian people and of Britain, that those who will have the final decision on the recommendations which the Commission will put forward should possess some clear conception of the achievements of the British in India, the complexity of the Indian problem as it exists to-day, and the danger of embarking on ill-considered experiments in a country which, so far from being homogeneous, is unhappily rent by communal and religious differences. The Government of India Act of 1919, which embodied the present Constitution, was passed with unanimity by Parliament. But it is hardly too much to say that very few members of the House of Commons realised the implications of the changes to which they assented with the generous hope that they were inaugurating a new era of contentment for India. And how many members of the present House could give an intelligible account of the events which have passed in that country since the Reforms came into operation? The ideas of the British electorate on Indian affairs are admittedly nebulous, and yet it is they who will have the last word in any fresh decision that may be made.

In the following pages it will be sought to show that India has derived inestimable benefits from the British connection; that the administration of India to-day, while sharing the imperfections inherent in all human institutions, is inspired by honesty of purpose and high ideals of duty; and that any weakening of the links which join the destinies of Britain and India would be pregnant with evil possibilities for both countries. The working of the Reformed Constitution will also be examined and the genesis of the many outbreaks of violence that have occurred in recent years will be discussed.

Evidence will, moreover, be cited to illustrate the difficulties which British administrators have had to face in the past owing to the prevalence of deep-rooted customs inconsistent with social and economic progress, and to show that these customs still form a grave obstacle to India's advance in material prosperity.

The Royal Commission on Agriculture in India, presided over by the Marquis of Linlithgow, has made many important recommendations for increasing the agricultural wealth of the country and raising the status of the cultivator. The Commission's voluminous report, which will be briefly discussed, shows evidence of painstaking enquiry and well-balanced judgment, and while the picture of village life in India which it presents is familiar to British officers who have worked in the districts, the facts put forward deserve far wider publicity than is afforded by the pages of a Blue Book. It is evident that the provision of great financial resources would be necessary in order to give full effect to the Commission's recommendations, and objection to enhanced taxation is more pronounced in India than in countries where the fiscal burdens of the people are much more onerous. It may be hoped, however, that the proposals made will bear fruit in time, and in any event the Commission has been able to focus attention on the real and vital problems of the Indian masses. The Indian villager possesses many attractive qualities, and British officers who have served India, and indeed all who know the hard-working peasant, will sincerely trust that his lot in life may be made easier as a result of the labours of the Commission.

The attitude of the Swarajists towards the enquiry has been characteristic. The Commission was made the subject of a gibe by the political head of the party when it was appointed, and upon the presentation of its report the leading Swarajist journal declared that it had been called into being with the ulterior motive of causing a set-back to the non-co-operation movement and creating a cleavage between the classes and the masses. It was also, according to this veracious commentator, intended to find ways and means to supply British manufacturers with India's raw materials and "to give the British customer his daily foodstuffs." The Commission, it may be observed, included four Indian members of standing and repute.

I

A MYTHICAL INDIA

" I see in some quarters a disposition again to-day to repeat what I regard as the nonsensical statement, that when the British first went to India they found her united and prosperous, and that they have made her to-day poor and disunited. It would be impossible to find in any connection so complete a travesty of the facts of history."—EARL WINTERTON, *Under-Secretary of State for India, in the House of Commons, July* 9, 1925.

THE legend of a Golden Age of India which ended with the advent of the British has no foundation. Nor is there any basis in fact for the assertion that an idyllic system of village government existed until it was destroyed by the newcomers from Europe. The evidence available regarding the lot of the people of India during the centuries which preceded the rise of the British power shows that the masses were steeped in misery.

There was splendour in the palace of the ruler and hopeless poverty in the hut of the peasant. Pelsart, the head of the Dutch factory at Agra, writing in 1626, declared that the life of the people could not adequately be described, " for here is the home of stark want and the dwelling-place of bitter woe." The statu~ of workmen, peasants and shopkeepers, he said, differed very little from voluntary slavery. If an Imperial officer wanted a workman, the man was not asked if he were willing to come, but was seized in his house, or in the street, well beaten if he should dare to raise any objection, and in the evening paid half his wages, or perhaps nothing at all. The shopkeepers, according to Pelsart, were better off than the workmen, and some of them were even well-to-do. But they must not let the fact be seen, or they would be the victims of trumped-up charges and their property would be legally confiscated, for informers swarmed like flies round the officials, perjuring themselves when necessary in order to remain in favour. Bernier, writing in the second half of the seventeenth century, stated that even a considerable proportion of good land remained untilled owing to want of labourers, many of whom perished in consequence of the bad treatment they experienced from their governors. Mr. W. H. Moreland, whose careful researches are of profound value to the student of Indian history, thus describes the position: "Weavers, naked themselves, toiled to clothe others. Peasants, themselves hungry, toiled to feed the towns and cities. India, taken as a unit, parted with useful commodities in exchange for gold and silver, or, in other words gave bread for stones. Men and women, living from season to season on the verge of hunger, could be contented so long as the supply of food held out . when it failed, as it so often did, their hope of salvation was the slave-trader, and the alternatives were cannibalism, suicide or starvation. The only way of escape from that system lay through an increase in production, but this road was barred effectively by the administrative methods in vogue, which penalised production and regarded every indication of increased consumption as a signal for fresh extortion." The many famines which afflicted India during the seventeenth century were attended with indescribable horrors.

Another Dutch trader, van Twist, has left a poignant narrative of the devastation caused over large tracts of the country owing to the failure of the rains. In the great famine of 1630-31 starvation drove people to cannibalism in Gujerat. Men deserted their wives and children. Women sold themselves as slaves. Mothers sold their own offspring, and children, deserted by their parents, sold themselves. Whole families took poison and thus met a common death; others threw themselves into the rivers and so ended their misery. Even in the streets, and still more on journeys by road, men ran great danger of being murdered and eaten.

While the Mogul Empire was undergoing the process of dissolution, the miseries of the unhappy people were accentuated by the horrors of war.

The story is a harrowing one, and can only be touched upon here. In 1739 Nadir Shah, the Persian conqueror, descended from the North and captured the Imperial City of Delhi. During the Persian occupation a rumour was spread abroad that Nadir Shah was dead. This report led to a rising of the inhabitants, whereupon the Persian king ordered a general massacre which lasted for nine hours. After a stay of fifty-eight days in Delhi, he left for Persia, taking with him enormous wealth which had been extorted from all classes of the population. In 1757 Delhi was again the scene of massacre and plunder, the Durrani Afghan, Ahmad Shah, having invaded India and adopted the traditional methods of the victors of that day. A curious example of the grotesque exaggeration of modern political oratory was provided in recent years by a member of the Indian Legislature, who, in denouncing a measure of which he did not approve, compared the Government of India to Nadir Shah.

With the extension of the British power large areas of country were freed from the excesses of marauders. But it was long before the whole of India emerged from the welter of rapine and war. The early part of the nineteenth century was marked by conflicts between the British and the Marathas, and Calcutta has a reminder in the Maratha Ditch of the raids of these fierce horsemen into Bengal. It is noteworthy that during this period the inhabitants of territories outside the areas subject to the British, who had suffered from the oppression and cruelties of plundering bands, declared that they had a right to British protection. The directors of the East India Company, so far from desiring to extend their jurisdiction, were averse from accepting fresh responsibilities. But the consequence of their policy of non-intervention created an impossible situation.

In 1816 the widespread depredations of the Pindaris impelled the Governor-General, Lord Hastings, to decisive action. The Pindaris, who first settled in Central India, were banditti of the most ferocious type. Their greed and cruelty defied description. They descended in bands, sometimes numbering several thousands, upon towns and villages, committed unspeakable outrages and destroyed what property they could not carry away. A climax was reached when they raided in force the East India Company's territory in the Northern Sircars. It is recorded that during this raid they plundered 339 villages, killed 182 persons and tortured 3,600 others. On receiving reports of their atrocities Lord Hastings, deeply moved by the harrowing stories which had reached him, decided that stern measures must be resorted to in order to end an intolerable evil. In his Journal, which was subsequently published, the Governor-General cited a letter he had received describing the horrors experienced by the people of the Guntur Sircar. A village was surrounded by Pindaris, and terrified by the fate that had befallen the people of other districts, the men decided upon the desperate expedient of burning themselves with their wives and children. Hundreds of women in other villages, unable to endure existence after the infamies they had suffered, put an end to their lives. All the young girls were carried off, "tied three or four together like calves on a horse to be sold."

In order to suppress the Pindaris and to cope with any developments that might follow systematic operations against these marauders, an army of some 120,000 men was mobilised, including 13,000 Europeans. The campaign was pursued with relentless vigour, and by the early part of 1818 organised opposition by the Pindaris had come to an end. But the operations undertaken led to a fierce conflict with the Marathas, with whom the Pindaris had had close relations, and the campaign terminated in a settlement which ensured British supremacy in the Maratha country.

It was with no visions of territorial aggrandisement that the British originally entered into relations with India. The East India Company was a body of merchant adventurers; its primary object was the purchase of Indian goods and their sale in Europe. The export trade in Indian merchandise which it thus established was of direct benefit to the Indian producer as well as to the Company.

While the directors of the East India Company set their faces against the intervention of their servants in Indian affairs, the unsettled state of the country and the chaos arising from internecine warfare made a continuation of this attitude impossible. Hence the creation of what is now the Indian Empire. The most recent extension of British rule dates from 1856, when the annexation of Oudh was decided upon in consequence of the prevalence in that kingdom of terrible and growing misrule. The Punjab had been annexed by Lord Dalhousie in 1849. He resorted to this step on the ground that it was necessary for the establishment of peace over an extensive area. There was, he said, no government in the Punjab, and if he had not proclaimed a distinct policy, the country would have fallen into a state of disturbance and utter anarchy. The prosperity of the Punjab to-day, after less than eighty years of British administration, testifies to the wisdom and the energy of those who have participated in the work of reconstruction and development.

II

BRITISH MEASURES OF DELIVERANCE

"YET such things exist after 150 years of British rule"—how often is this the prelude to a dissertation on the sins of omission and commission of the administrators of India. It may possibly be that the cold weather critics from England who after a brief tour through India find so little to commend in our administration and so much to condemn, could, if subjected to cross-examination, give an intelligible account of the extent of British rule in that country a century and a half ago. But it is charitable to assume that they are not familiar with the obstacles which a handful of British officials had to face before they could even begin to provide India with amenities now regarded as elementary in settled countries of the West. Some years ago an eminent English physician was called in to treat an Indian ruler who had been attacked by a stubborn disease. Most friendly relations existed between the physician and his distinguished patient, but the Prince became restive owing to the slowness of his recovery, and in the end the Englishman was impelled to say with a sigh, "What the Maharaja wants is a magician, and I am only a doctor."

If British officials had been magicians they might have brought India up to the standard demanded by their critics. But they are only men, and as men they are to be judged. They have made mistakes and miscalculations, but of their work in India as a whole their countrymen have no reason to be ashamed.

Less than a century has passed since Lord William Bentinck penned his famous pronouncement on *suttee*, a rite which involved the immolation of Hindu widows on the funeral pyres of their husbands. The Government as it existed in the early years of the nineteenth century has been charged with timidity in permitting that terrible practice to continue. The critics may have been right, but it is clear from the words of Lord William Bentinck himself, that grave apprehension existed in many minds lest a measure which was opposed to the deep-rooted convictions of the Hindus might precipitate an upheaval that would prove disastrous in its results. Even that enlightened Indian reformer Raja Ram Mohan Roy expressed the opinion to the Governor-General that the practice might be suppressed quietly and unobservedly by placing increased difficulties in the way of its observance and by the indirect agency of the police. He feared that any public enactment would give rise to general unrest, and that the reasoning would be: "While the English were contending for power, they deemed it politic to allow universal toleration and to respect our religion, but having obtained the supremacy, their first act is a violation of their profession, and the next will probably be, like the Mahomedan conquerors, to force upon us their own religion." Lord William Bentinck happily was convinced that the abolition of *suttee* would appeal to enlightened Hindus, and that when the excitement caused by his decision to abolish it had passed away the Hindu community would "see that there can be no inconsistency in the ways of Providence, that to the command received as divine by all races of men 'No innocent blood shall be spilt,' there can be no exception." It could not, he said, be a dishonest ambition that the Government of which he formed part "should have the credit of an act which is to wash out a foul stain upon British rule and to stay the sacrifice of humanity and justice to a doubtful expediency." He felt that he would be guilty of little less than "multiplied murder" if he hesitated to perform the solemn obligation that lay upon him.

The fears of widespread troubles as a result of the prohibition proved to be unfounded. The opposition in Bengal took a more characteristic form. A deputation of Bengali gentlemen waited upon Lord William to express their strong dissent, but obtained no satisfaction from him. Meanwhile a committee of protest had been formed, and over eight hundred signatures were appended to a petition to the Privy Council for the restoration of *suttee.* Raja Ram Mohan Roy, who had proceeded to England, threw all his great influence into the opposition to the appeal, and the Privy Council, after listening to the eloquent arguments of the lawyers against "interference with liberty of conscience," rejected the petition.

The edict abolishing *suttee* throughout what then constituted British India came into operation in December, 1829. In the previous year there had been 464 cases of the immolation of Hindu widows in Bengal, where the practice was widely prevalent; indeed, as Mr. Edward Thompson states in his interesting study of the subject, there were instances of the burning of a score or even two score women with one quite unimportant man. But the rite continued to be practised in large areas in Northern and Western India which were outside British jurisdiction. The policy of the Government henceforth was described in Lord Dalhousie's famous minute of 1856, in which he reviewed his administration of India. In the time of those who preceded him, he said, great progress had been made in persuading all Indian princes to unite in denouncing the rite and in punishing those who should disregard the prohibition. The Government of India, since 1848, had only to follow up the measures of preceding years. When *suttee* occurred in an independent State, no opportunity of remonstrating had been lost. When it had occurred in any district within British control, no indulgence had been shown to the culprits.

It is disconcerting to find that cases of *suttee* still occur from time to time. Mr. E. C. Allen, late of the Indian Civil Service, recently described a notorious instance at Mainpuri, in the Agra Division, which took place in 1913. Mr. Allen, who was then a Sessions Judge, tried and sentenced a number of the men who were charged with having aided and abetted in the crime. The defence attempted to show that the accused were passive spectators; that neither they, the widow, nor anyone else had fired the funeral pyre, which was set alight by mysterious fire from heaven. More recently still, in June, 1928, the Patna High Court had before it the appeals of ten men who had been sentenced by a Sessions Judge to various terms of imprisonment for abetting in a case of *suttee*, and for unlawful assembly. The evidence was to the effect that a young Brahman woman had followed the body of her husband to a burning ghat on the banks of the Ganges, announcing her intention of performing *suttee*. The police vainly sought to dissuade her from her purpose, and when the inspector threatened to arrest her, the widow's relatives undertook to take her back to her village. This, however, proved to be a ruse on their part; the woman was conveyed instead to the burning ghat, and when the police again sought to intervene they met with threats from the accused men. The crowd by this time numbered about 5,000 and, regarding the situation as out of hand, the inspector decided not to make the arrest. Accordingly, after bathing in the Ganges, the widow seated herself on her husband's pyre, and soon afterwards her clothes burst out into flames. As no one had been seen by the people to apply a light to the pyre, the crowd believed they had witnessed a miracle and raised the cry of "Glory to *Suttee*." The woman later leaped into the river, and after attempts on the part of the police to rescue her had been frustrated, she left the water of her own accord and was taken to a hospital where she died.

It is regarded as inconceivable that *suttee* would again become an established custom if it were no longer a criminal offence. The history of the rite and of its suppression, however, tends to illustrate the nature of the problems with which the administrators of British India had to grapple, and provides an eloquent commentary on many of the impatient and uninformed criticisms of our administration.

Another task which fell to the lot of the British was the suppression of the *Thags*, the most evil association of criminals that ever afflicted India.

These men, who were banded together for the purpose of murdering and robbing peaceful travellers, claimed that in perpetrating most atrocious crimes they were performing a religious duty. The famous Colonel Sleeman, who played a leading part in their suppression and interrogated many of them in prison, declared that "there is not among them one who doubts the divine origin of the system of *Thuggee*, not one who doubts that he and all who have followed the trade of murder with the prescribed rites and observances were acting under the immediate orders and auspices of the Goddess Devee, Durga, Kalee or Bhawanee, as she is indifferently called, and consequently there is not one who feels the slightest remorse for the murders which he may, in the course of his vocation, have perpetrated or assisted in perpetrating. . . . He meditates his murders without any misgivings, he perpetrates them without any emotions of pity, and he remembers them without any feelings of remorse."

The history of the *Thags* and of the methods they employed as recounted by Sleeman is a terrible record of depravity and crime. For many years up to 1829, when their suppression was decided upon by Lord William Bentinck, the *Thags* traversed every great and frequented road from the Himalayas to the Nerbudda river, and from the Ganges to the Indus. What they regarded as religious rites preceded their crimes, and sacrifices to their goddess followed the murder and burial of their victims. The methods they pursued was to traverse the country in gangs of ostensibly peaceful wayfarers, and to accompany on the road the travellers whom they had selected as their victims. Often they would spend days with the unfortunate people in order to gain their confidence. Then, when the appointed spot had been reached, the *Thags* would suddenly fall upon the doomed persons and strangle them with a cord or cloth. Owing to the murders of sepoys on the road by *Thags*, the Commander-in-Chief was impelled to issue an Army Order warning Indian soldiers to be on their guard against the wiles of strangers who sought their company when they were proceeding on leave to visit their families.

The disturbed state of the country had long facilitated the operations of these criminals, and though in the earlier years of the nineteenth century a number of gangs had been broken up, difficulty was often experienced in securing the conviction of the members. Lord William Bentinck, feeling that the time had come when the *Thags* must be relentlessly put down as a danger to the community decided upon an extensive plan of operations to that end. Captain Sleeman, as he then was, was appointed General Superintendent for the Suppression of *Thag* Associations, and in the course of six years the work proved successful. Two thousand *Thags* had been arrested and tried; 1,500 convicted and sentenced to death or transportation. In 167 trials the prisoners were charged with the murder of 947 persons, but Sleeman affirmed that the murders for which the assassins were actually indicted "were not commonly more than a hundredth part of the murders they have perpetrated in the course of their career of crime."

British officers engaged in the suppression of the *Thags* remarked that it was painful to observe that landholders of every description were found ready to receive the murderers under their protection, from the desire to share the fruits of their expeditions. The secrecy which attended the nefarious operations of the *Thags* is well illustrated by a statement made by Sleeman himself. A few years prior to the commencement of the systematic suppression of the gangs he was in civil charge of a district in the valley of the Nerbudda, and he was convinced during this period that no ordinary robbery or theft could be committed without his becoming acquainted with it. Yet it was subsequently discovered that a gang of assassins lived within four hundred yards of his court, and that the extensive groves of a village only one stage away was one of the greatest places of murder in all India. The bodies of one hundred travellers who had fallen victims to the *Thags* lay buried in and around the groves of Mundesur.

III

CAUSES OF INDIAN POVERTY

"Our industrial schools, our experimental farms, our co-operative banks and numerous endeavours at economic uplift prove that we are keenly alive to the need of helping India to get bread. But a great unbiassed economist came to the conclusion that 'almost every economic ill in India is rooted in religious and social custom.' Every time you try to lift India economically, you run into a custom that baulks you."—"*The Christ of the Indian Road,*" *by the* Rev. Stanley Jones (*an American missionary*).

We have seen that the deliverance of India from internal warfare was not completely effected until comparatively recent times. That deliverance, in itself, was an inestimable blessing to the common people. The suppression of *suttee*, the extirpation of the *Thags* and the establishment of security from famine are among the notable achievements of British rule. India, indeed, is advancing in material prosperity, but the task of improving the economic position of the masses and of promoting their physical welfare presents difficulties which are beyond the conception of those who are not familiar with Indian conditions. The population of British India is nearly 250 millions, of whom the vast majority are dependent on agriculture, and live in the 498,527 villages which are scattered throughout a vast sub-continent. If this great population were homogeneous and animated by an intelligent desire for material progress the task of the administrators of the country would be enormously simplified. Not only is that aspiration absent, but the greater part of the inhabitants of India are wedded to customs which present a formidable barrier to their prosperity and a grave obstacle to the improvement of the public health.

Nearly 700 out of every 1,000 of the population are Hindus, and the objection of the Hindu to the taking of life leads to the destruction of a substantial proportion of the crops by wild animals and birds. The monkey and the peacock and his harem enjoy special immunity on religious grounds. Plague, which is a terrible source of disease and death, is caused by the rat flea, and the black rat, which is the source of infection, consumes grain to the value of at least £16 million annually.

Yet Major Norman White, of the Indian Medical Service, an eminent authority on plague, declared in an official report to the Government of India, that of all preventable diseases none is more preventable than is bubonic plague. "If educated people," he wrote, "would unite in an effort to inculcate far and wide some idea of the significance of the statement that ten million people in India have fallen victims to plague; of the economic loss that India has suffered from the ravages of plague; of the wholesale disorganization to which industry is liable for several months in severe plague years; of the absolute dependence of plague epidemics on rat infestation, and of the very considerable financial loss suffered as a result of the depredations of rats, the Indian plague problem would find a ready solution."

The report of the Royal Commission on Agriculture in India directs attention to two curious facts related to the problem under discussion. In dealing with sericulture, the report points out that where silkworms can be reared a valuable subsidiary industry is available to the villager; the more so that it provides what is essentially a spare-time occupation. In certain areas and amongst certain classes, however, there are religious prejudices against the processes this industry involves. In regard to the development of a poultry industry, which would be of great value to the consumer and to the cultivator alike, similar prejudices exist, though some evidence is available to show that these prejudices are not incapable of being overcome. Mr. Hubert Calvert, a member of the Commission, again, in his valuable work, *The Wealth and Prosperity of the Punjab*, remarks that the growing of vegetables is looked upon in that Province as degrading to a real agriculturist, and that *malis* (market gardeners) are actually giving up vegetables for wheat cultivation in order to raise their social status.

Great economic loss arises from the Hindu veneration for the cow. The provision of an adequate supply of milk at a comparatively low price would be a valuable boon to India, and would prove a factor in reducing infant mortality. The yield of milk from the average Indian cow is extremely low, and the religious tenets of the people constitute an obstacle to the improvement of the breed and also lead to the consumption by animals of no economic value of fodder which is badly needed for useful cattle. It has been estimated by a competent authority that the number of these useless animals is not less than 14,000,000 and that in the course of six years, which is taken as their average life, they consume fodder of an aggregate value of about £100,000,000.

A census taken in 1924-5 gave the total number of cattle and buffaloes in British India as 151 millions. The average Indian cow is a poor emaciated creature owing to the methods adopted by the agriculturist in dealing with his stock. In India, the Royal Commission on Agriculture remark, the custom that an animal not actually working should find its food in the jungle when there is no fodder available renders it unusual for the owner to make any sacrifice for the well-being of his cattle. Shortage of fodder is often accentuated by droughts. It is suggested that fear of loss by disease, moreover, causes many cultivators to keep more stock than is necessary, a custom which increases the difficulty of providing a proper supply of fodder. Lord Linlithgow and his colleagues, after exhaustive enquiry, arrived at the conclusion that India has acquired so large a cattle population, and the size of the animals in many areas is so small, that the task of arresting the process of deterioration and of improving the breed has become a gigantic one. Yet all who have studied the subject will agree with their pronouncement that the prosperity of Indian agriculture is largely dependent on the improvement of the country's cattle.

The loss of cattle through disease must be a crushing burden. It is one of the main causes of borrowing on usurious terms from the village moneylender. Rinderpest is a most fruitful source of cattle mortality, but the methods of stamping out this scourge which have proved successful in European countries cannot be utilised in the Indian villages owing to the religious beliefs of the bulk of the cultivators. In the Punjab alone between £2,250,000 and £3,000,000 annually is believed to be lost through preventable cattle disease.

The agricultural indebtedness of India has been estimated at from £400,000,000 to £500,000,000 sterling, on which very high rates of interest are usually paid. The cultivator regards debt rather as a permanent feature of his life than as an unfortunate incident. That his indebtedness may partially be due to his legitimate requirements is true, but as has already been shown, mortality among his cattle frequently drives the villager to the moneylender, and cattle mortality could be materially reduced. Extravagant expenditure on ceremonial occasions is a common cause of indebtedness. On the occasion of a wedding, for instance, a man will borrow a sum equal, perhaps, to more than the whole family income for a year, and he may spend the remainder of his life in trying to satisfy the claims of the lender.

The evidence in support of the improvidence of the unfortunate cultivator is overwhelming; it has been emphasised by many investigators whose knowledge and judgment are beyond dispute. In 1892, after having examined the assessment papers of over 9,000 villages in the Central Provinces, Sir J. B. Fuller found that indebtedness arose from "sheer wastefulness and extravagance."

Mr. K. L. Datta, who carried out an enquiry into the rise in prices in India, in a report issued in 1915, again, wrote: "In a good year his (the cultivator's) ignorance and improvidence make him spend the whole of his surplus on marriages and festivities, and his extravagance on such occasions often leads him even in good years to the doors of the moneylender. A ryat would stop at no extravagance in marrying one of his children or performing any funeral or social ceremony, to show more ostentation than his fellows." The Famine Commission of 1880 arrived at the conclusion that, in the Punjab, expenditure on marriage and other ceremonies was one of the most prominent causes of indebtedness. This problem is the subject of an illuminating chapter in Mr. M. L. Darling's notable book, *The Punjab Peasant in Prosperity and Debt*. The writer, a well-known member of the Indian Civil Service, and an eminent authority on rural economics, cites a case within his own knowledge where a co-operator spent Rs. 1,300 on marrying a son, and Rs. 400 in the next year on marrying a daughter. These combined amounts represented 17 years' rental of his holding of 10 acres; and what made it worse was that he was already in debt to the extent of Rs. 1,500.

It seems clear that the non-productive portion of the debt of the agriculturist is very much greater than the productive portion, and where the cultivator's holding has increased in value owing to the construction of irrigation works and railways, the facilities for extravagant borrowing offered to him constitute a temptation which he is often unable to resist. The alarming rate at which land was being transferred from the possession of the agricultural classes to the hands of moneylenders has led in several Provinces to the passing of legislation to check that undesirable process, but the process still continues, and the Linlithgow Commission has definitely expressed the opinion that enquiry should once more be instituted into the extent to which the hereditary cultivating class is being expropriated by those who do not themselves cultivate the land.

In Bihar and Orissa a system prevails by which landlords, in return for a loan, secure the services of a labourer for life, and as a fresh loan is granted on the occasion of the marriage of his son, the condition of servitude becomes hereditary. Legislation directed against this system has not so far proved effective, and further measures appear to be essential if the system is to be suppressed.

The wealth of the Indian moneylender is proverbial. In the Punjab, which, under British administration, has become the richest agricultural Province in the country, it is estimated that the 40,000 moneylenders derive an aggregate income of between £6,000,000 and £9,000,000 from the people. The economic loss of the Province through litigation is placed at about £3,000,000.

The passion for litigation which is so prevalent in India may, indeed, be cited as a cause of grave economic evils. A rich Indian will "run" a lawsuit for sport, just as a rich Englishman will run a racehorse; while among the agricultural masses a case in the Courts gives a spice of excitement to life. Unscrupulous persons take advantage of this weakness of the people and foment disputes for their own pecuniary gain. In a large proportion of the civil suits the amount actually in dispute is small; in 1925, for instance, over a million of these suits were for sums of less than 50 rupees. But the total cost to the community is a very serious matter; in the Punjab, it is estimated that some 2,500,000 persons attend the courts in a normal year, and that the loss of time is not less than ten million days. In fact, as Mr. Calvert has observed, "If the time, energy, intelligence and skill devoted to litigation could be diverted to medical relief, one of the biggest problems of the Province would be solved." Many of the suits arise from the claims of moneylenders, and a vicious circle is established, since litigation constitutes a fruitful source of borrowing. Meanwhile the legal fraternity grows in numbers and in wealth. Thirty-two years ago there were 360 lawyers in the Punjab; to-day there are over 1,200, and the number is apparently still increasing. Mr. Darling refers to a case which vividly illustrates the trivial causes from which litigation arises and the ruinous results which may follow. A villager, in a moment of absentmindedness, allowed his bullocks to stray into his neighbour's crops. The neighbour appearing on the scene, there was the inevitable volley of abuse followed up by blows, which, however, did no great harm. The injured party resorted to the police, and paid Rs. 45 to have the case registered, as it was a trivial affair with which the police had no concern. His next step was to obtain a certificate from the local sub-assistant surgeon that serious injuries had been inflicted, but, as the damage done was small, Rs. 190 had to be paid before the certificate was forthcoming. Alarmed at the issue of the certificate the other party bestirred himself and commenced spending money to obtain evidence to rebut the charge. At this stage, before proceedings in court had been commenced, Mr. Darling's informant intervened and succeeded in compromising the case, which ended in mutual apologies and an expenditure of Rs. 409.

The report of the Civil Justice Committee, appointed by Lord Reading, provides a mass of astonishing information regarding the abuse of the law courts. The persistence with which an Indian, even of the enlightened classes, will follow up a suit from court to court is amazing. Colonel B. O. Roe, formerly a District and Sessions Judge, who was a co-opted member of the Commission, once asked an Indian country gentleman why he had taken a case to the High Court when he had no possible chance of success. His reply was that his *izzat* demanded it. *Izzat* is an expression which it is difficult to translate. The nearest word in use in this country is perhaps prestige: Sir Walter Lawrence, in *The India we Served*, defines it as "honour, repute and the world's esteem." Colonel Roe relates an incident which indicates what *izzat* means to the Indian. At a garden party which he attended there was an Indian gentleman who was the centre of considerable interest. On enquiring the reason, Colonel Roe was told that he had just had a lawsuit which was carried to the Privy Council. Did he win it? Colonel Roe asked. "Oh, no, he lost all right," was the reply. "But think of the *izzat*, a case before the Privy Council."

The "fragmentation" of holdings, due to the laws of inheritance, is another obstacle to agricultural prosperity. Under the laws in question, on the death of the head of a family the land he possessed is distributed among his sons, and this process ultimately leads to extraordinary results. In the Punjab there are fields over a mile long and only a few yards wide, and cases have been discovered where a villager's holding was situated in two hundred different places. Sometimes the process of sub-division has been carried so far that cultivation of the land has actually become unprofitable.

India has been a sink of the precious metals from time immemorial; the hoarding of gold and silver or their conversion into ornaments has deprived the country of the capital which might have been utilised for productive purposes and have given a great stimulus to industrial prosperity. The drain of gold and silver to the East, indeed, is mentioned by the writers of the later Roman Empire, and it was a matter of adverse comment in England in the seventeenth and eighteenth centuries. In recent years this practice has led to strong opposition being offered to the establishment of a gold currency in India, based on the fear that the coins would either be hoarded or melted down, and that the consequent accentuation of the drain on the world's gold resources would lead to the restriction of banking credit in Western countries, a development which would react on India's trade prosperity. Some idea of the extent of the absorption of the precious metals by India may be gathered from the fact that the net imports of gold in 1924-25 amounted to about 74 crores of rupees, or over £55,000,000 at the present rate of exchange, and the corresponding imports of silver to 20 crores or £15,000,000. These figures are a suitable commentary on the complaint that India is wretchedly poor and also on the rhetorical flights of that section of Indian politicians who incessantly denounce the "exploitation" of the country by British capitalists. The truth is that India is possessed of enormous natural resources, and that if the wealth sunk in hoards or converted into ornaments had been intelligently applied to industrial development there would have been no necessity for the importation of capital from abroad. As it is, India owes her railway system, her irrigation works, and her jute, coal and tea industries to British enterprise, the only major industries established by Indians being cotton manufacturing, mainly in the Bombay Presidency, and the Tata Iron and Steel works at Jamshedpur. The jute industry has been of great value to the cultivators of Bengal, while the tea gardens have provided profitable employment for hundreds of thousands of landless labourers and given them opportunities of advancement which they would never have enjoyed in the over-populated areas in which they were born.

Within the past few years it has been possible to raise Government loans within the country. Indians have, moreover, acquired large interests in jute mills through the purchase of shares, and they are also beginning to concern themselves in the cultivation of tea. These signs augur well for the future, and are welcomed alike by the Government of India and by the British mercantile community.

In discussions on public health, critics who point to the high rate of mortality in India usually take no account of factors beyond the control of Government which foster disease and hasten death. The seclusion of women, the custom of early marriage, and the practices followed at childbirth exercise a potent influence in increasing mortality. These questions have been freely ventilated of late, and it is not necessary to enlarge upon them here. The insanitary condition of the water supplies of the villages, which might be remedied by the people themselves, is also a serious drawback to the health of the rural population, while the immunity too often enjoyed by the black rat, which spreads bubonic plague, adds to the death rate. The evidence given before the Linlithgow Commission on this subject by Lieut.-Colonel Grahame, Public Health Commissioner with the Government of India, is of especial interest. Colonel Grahame expressed the belief that it was doubtful whether any Government in the world could show a better record of State aid in regard to medical education and medical relief than the Government of India. "In the matter of public health, however," he declared, "we are at once up against the rooted prejudices of a highly conservative congeries of people in whom, in many instances, religious practices enter largely into domestic affairs, especially in regard to illness and nutrition. It will, therefore, be readily understood why the deliberate policy of Government in public health matters should have been to lead rather than to compel, and to propagate with a view to creating in time a public health conscience."

Educated Indians gratefully recognise the value of the services rendered to their country by Western medical scientists. The work of Sir Ronald Ross in regard to malaria and that of Sir Leonard Rogers in regard to cholera and leprosy are famous throughout the scientific world, and, with other achievements of members of the Indian Medical Service, have proved of incalculable benefit to India.

IV

A RECORD OF PROGRESS

"We wish for the Indians immunity from famine and pestilence, steady progress in agriculture and industry, and a safe and material advance in social conditions."—*His Majesty The King Emperor.*

THE British administrators of India would have been inhuman if they had supinely tolerated the ills which afflict the Indian masses. So far from adopting an attitude of indifference, the members of the Indian Civil Service and those who have served India as Viceroys and Governors have worked strenuously for the people, and though blunders in policy have been made, the devotion of the district officer to the peasantry has never wavered. In times of famine and pestilence the members of the Indian Services have worked with untiring fidelity among the people, even unto death, and the efforts made by the "bureaucracy" to rescue the cultivator from debt and to secure to him protection from oppression, deserve generous appreciation from their fellow countrymen. Even to-day, when the disseminators of anti-British slanders are incessant in their attacks on the Services, the district officer over large areas of country possesses the confidence and even the affection of the peasantry whom he serves, and it is the pens of British officials that have provided the most illuminating literature on the troubles, the difficulties and the needs of the villager. The work of administration is now being shared in an increasing degree by Indians, and, notably in the security Services, Indian officers have shown courage and fortitude which could not be surpassed by men of any other race. It must be remembered that the Indian Civil Service comprises a very small number of men, considering the enormous extent of the country and the vast population committed to its charge. It now consists of 1,250 members in all, of whom 330 are Indians, while the population of British India, as we have seen, is nearly 250,000,000.

In India, moreover, Government is expected to initiate and to carry out every movement for the advancement of the people in material prosperity, for the improvement of agriculture, for education and for the preservation of the public health. The wealthy landlord who seeks to promote the interests of agriculture by example and by precept is a *rara avis*. Men of education, moreover, are seldom found in the villages. This fact was emphasised by the members of the Linlithgow Commission, who wrote in their report: "He (the villager) lacks leadership. No one corresponding to the squire, the doctor and the parson is to be found in an Indian village. The educated man is not willing to live his life in a village except in a few rare cases where ideals of service overcome the absence of social amenities."

The great majority of the vocal politicians in India are townsmen who possess no acquaintance with rural conditions; hence the minor part that agriculture plays in the Central Legislature. In my long experience of the Indian Legislative Assembly I can remember only one measure bearing directly on agriculture introduced by a Swarajist member. This was a Bill for the prohibition of the export of cattle. The statement of "Objects and Reasons" attached, it was remarked at the time, was reminiscent of *Alice in Wonderland*. It set out that "India is an agricultural country," a truism to which no objection could be taken; nor could the statement be challenged that "cattle are essential to the agriculturist and milk to the great bulk of the population." But the assertion which followed was calculated to excite derision: "A large number of cattle has of late been exported every year for the purpose of the trade. This has naturally appreciably raised the prices of cattle and milk. The scarcity of milk is a serious hardship upon the people in general, but its evil results have been most felt in the case of infants.

The great rise in infant mortality during recent years has been distressing. The object of this Bill is to combat these growing evils to some extent by penalising export trade in cattle." Now in the previous year the number of cattle, not necessarily milch cows, exported was 12,600, equal to one head for every 40 villages in India. The idea that these exports were seriously diminishing the milk supply of the country was so ludicrous that nothing more was heard of the Bill. The actual cause of the inadequacy of the milk supply is the low producing capacity of the Indian cow, the average yield of which during the lactation period is 800 lbs., compared with the 12,000 lbs. given by some of the cross-bred animals produced at the Imperial Agricultural Institute at Pusa. It is in this direction that the solution of the problem of the milk supply lies, yet the remedy proposed by the Swarajist townsman was the imprisonment for six months of anyone convicted of the heinous crime of exporting a single head of cattle, a similar penalty to be inflicted on anyone who abetted him.

It has long been realised that measures for improving agriculture in India must fail to achieve their full purpose unless the cultivator is freed from the burden of unproductive debt. This problem is one of great difficulty and complexity, but there is reason to hope that it is capable of solution through the agency of the system of co-operative credit. The people themselves, except where the co-operative credit society has made its influence felt, accept their heavy indebtedness, with its evil concomitants, as in the natural order of affairs; they are unversed themselves in business methods, and, as we have seen, educated men of public spirit are seldom found in the villages. The moneylender naturally regarded the incursion of the Government's officers into his domain with indignation and hostility; for his trade is one of the most profitable in India. Before the advent of co-operative credit he had the field to himself. He charged interest ranging up to 40 per cent., and even more, on his loans, and he added to his gains and to the indebtedness of the borrower by malpractices of the grossest kind. One of the commonest devices of the village moneylender was to deduct an anna in the rupee from the sum advanced and to charge interest on the full amount. He kept false books in order to cheat his victim, and resorted to other dishonest devices to fill his coffers.

The co-operative credit movement has been the means of delivering many a cultivator from the toils of the usurer, though the work yet to be accomplished is formidable. But the progress already achieved gives promise of much greater things in the future, and it is no exaggeration to say that the salvation of the Indian agriculturist lies in co-operation.

This beneficent movement was initiated by Government. The evils arising from rural indebtedness were tacitly acquiesced in by the community at large, for they had existed from time immemorial, and in the early stages of the co-operative credit society little support for the innovation was received from the educated classes. The first step towards inaugurating the movement was the decision of the Government of Madras to depute Sir Frederick Nicholson, one of its officers, to enquire into the working of co-operative credit societies in Europe. Sir Frederick's voluminous report was issued in two parts, the first in 1895 and the second in 1897, and it advocated the establishment of co-operative credit societies on the lines of those founded in Germany by Raiffeisen. Experimental societies were formed in the Punjab by Sir Edward Maclagan and Captain Crosthwaite, and in the United Provinces by Mr. Dupernex of the Indian Civil Service. These societies were constituted under the then existing company law, but, as a result of the recommendations of the Famine Commission of 1901, the Co-operative Credit Societies Act was passed in 1904, and active measures were taken to establish the movement on a broad basis. Members of the Indian Civil Service worked with assiduity to promote its success.

Valuable books showing an intimate knowledge of the troubles, the difficulties and the needs of the cultivator have been published by a number of these officials, notably by Mr. H. Calvert, Mr. M. L. Darling and Mr. C. F. Strickland of the Punjab, and the late Major Jack, who made a most interesting study of indebtedness in the Faridpur district of Bengal.

The progress of the movement is shown by the fact that there are now in existence in British India some 67,000 agricultural primary societies, with an aggregate capital of upwards of £18,000,000. The direct relief afforded by the provision of loans at moderate rates of interest is far from being the only benefit conferred by the establishment of the village society. Wherever the movement has taken root, the charges of the moneylender have been reduced, and a new vision of life has been made manifest to the people. Borrowing for non-productive purposes has been sternly discouraged by the members themselves; extravagant expenditure on marriage and other ceremonies is frowned upon, and drunkards and persons of bad character are refused admission to the societies. Money, moreover, has been voted by the societies for the purposes of education and sanitation. One of the main difficulties experienced in educating the rural population is found in the tendency of parents to remove their children from school before they have acquired sufficient book knowledge to be of any use to them in life. It is, therefore, of special interest that in the Punjab there are 158 co-operative societies with a membership of 7,000 parents, who have pledged themselves to send their children to school for four years continuously, or until they have attained the fourth standard.

The co-operative principle has been extended to other beneficent objects, though the provision of credit for the cultivator on moderate terms is recognised to be the most important function of the co-operative society to-day. The non-credit societies include organizations formed for the promotion of better farming and better living, for fighting malaria, for extending irrigation and for the improvement of the breeds of cattle. Others are devoted to the encouragement of education, to the sale of improved varieties of seed and to the marketing of produce. In Calcutta a co-operative milk union, to which a large number of rural societies are affiliated, has done valuable work both for the producer and the consumer.

A promising effort to check litigation in the Punjab, which is a curse to the Province, was inaugurated by Mr. Calvert, who then held the office of Registrar of Co-operative Societies. In order to enable the people to avoid resorting to the Courts at ruinous expense, Mr. Calvert formed arbitration societies, which proved a marked success. In 1922 there were 148 of these bodies in existence with nearly 17,000 members, and as the Civil Justice Committee remarked in their report, many of the cases decided related to cattle trespass and boundary disputes, trivial matters which, however, often lead to riots and costly proceedings in the courts. For some reason or other these societies were closed down by Ministerial order, but they have now been re-started and are said to number 27 and to possess a membership of 3,000.

An attempt has been made in the Central Provinces to deal with the problem of fragmentation of holdings by legislation, the Act rendering it possible for consolidation of holdings to be effected in certain areas where a majority of the landholders involved promote a scheme with that purpose in view. In the Punjab the Co-operative Credit Department has applied itself to the problem with substantial success. By means of patient and well-devised propaganda the officers of the Department have been able to induce the owners of many "fragmented" plots to agree to consolidation projects, although the difficulties, owing to the obduracy of short-sighted individuals among the cultivators involved, have frequently been formidable.

India owes a debt of gratitude to Lord Curzon for the deep personal interest he showed in the indebtedness of the peasantry and for having been instrumental in passing the Act which made possible the creation of the great network of co-operative credit societies that now exists. On the day that the Act came into operation he made an eloquent appeal to the Indian communities to utilise it for the benefit of the most deserving and helpless class in India. "Government," he said, "has played its part. I invite them to play theirs."

When he was leaving India Lord Curzon enumerated the principles by which he had been guided, prominent among these being regard for the welfare of "the Indian poor, the Indian peasant, the patient, humble, silent millions, the 80 per cent. who subsist by agriculture, who know very little of policies, but who profit or suffer by their results, and whom men's eyes, even the eyes of their countrymen, too often forget." Lord Curzon affirmed that the peasant "has been in the background of every policy for which I have been responsible, of every surplus of which I have assisted in the disposition."

The differences which arose between this great Viceroy and Lord Kitchener are still remembered; but how many people outside India have the slightest knowledge of the great measures inaugurated by Lord Curzon for the benefit of the Indian masses?

The East India Company, even in its earlier

days, devoted some attention to the improvement of crops in India. The promotion of agricultural research on an organised basis dates, however, from 1903, when Lord Curzon decided to establish the now famous Agricultural Research Institute at Pusa, in Bihar. It is worthy of note that a generous gift of £30,000 by Mr. Henry Phipps of Chicago, to be utilised for some object of public utility at Lord Curzon's discretion, was applied towards the cost of bringing the Pusa Institute into being. The scientific work carried on at Pusa and at the various establishments of the Provincial Agricultural Departments has substantially enhanced the income of the cultivating classes. So multifarious are the activities of the officers of Pusa and of the Departments that it is impossible to state in figures the value of their achievements. Some idea of what has been done is, however, to be obtained from the annual reviews of Dr. Clouston, Agricultural Adviser to the Government of India, which are full of encouragement for all who are concerned in the welfare of the Indian cultivator. Dr. Clouston's estimates of the value to the agriculturist of the improved varieties of crops introduced as a result of scientific research and experiment are invariably conservative, and as he himself admits, they undoubtedly understate the case. Still, in his latest review, he shows that, according to official statistics, there were in 1926-27, 8,816,000 acres sown with these new varieties, and taking the increased value of the resultant crops at Rs. 12, or eighteen shillings, per acre, an addition of some £8,000,000 was made in that year to the agricultural wealth of India. These figures do not, however, state the whole truth. The selected varieties are now so widely grown that departmental statistics no longer represent the extent to which they have spread, and many instances can be cited where a far greater increase in the average yield than Rs. 15 per acre is secured.

In the Central Provinces alone the spread of Roscum cotton has added crores of rupees (a crore is equivalent to £750,000) to the profits of the growers, and improved sugar canes introduced in the same Province have given 8,425 lbs. of *gur* (unrefined sugar) per acre against 4,440 lbs. formerly obtained. The introduction during 1926-27 of an improved variety of ground-nut in another area raised the value of the cultivators' crop from about eighteen shillings to £4 10s. 0d. per acre. In a recent year 600,000 acres sown with American cotton in the Punjab enhanced the value of the out-turn by nearly £2,000,000, and in Madras the introduction of Cambodia cotton enabled the cultivator to secure from £11 to £15 per acre from land which had previously given a return from £8 to £4 10s. per acre.

Again, the increased value of the yield of 1,400,000 acres of wheat grown from improved seed amounted in a single year to more than £2,000,000. The fame of the wheats produced at Pusa now extends far beyond the confines of India, and the varieties known as Pusa 4 and Pusa 12 have carried off first prizes at agricultural shows in Australia.

The scientific work for the improvement of Indian crops by the production of new varieties thus covers a wide range of agricultural products, affecting cultivation in every part of the country, and it is gratifying to observe that the area under these improved varieties has increased by 75 per cent. during the past three years, progress having been made at the rate of a million and a quarter acres per annum.

It has already been stated that the evolution of valuable crops is only one of the many beneficent activities of the agricultural officers. Unflagging attention is being devoted to checking the ravages of cattle disease and of insect pests, to the provision of better supplies of fodder, to the reclamation of saline lands, to the problem of fertilisers, to agricultural and veterinary education, to the improvement of the breeds of stock and to the introduction of more efficient agricultural implements. The annual loss from insect pests has been estimated at £135,000,000, so there is an enormous field here for the work of the scientist.

It is obvious that the inferiority of the average Indian bovine animal must be a serious obstacle to the economic progress of a country which is primarily dependent upon its agricultural industry. Constant efforts have, therefore, been made both at Pusa and at the Provincial stations to provide a remedy, and it has been shown to be possible to breed cows which yield from five to fifteen times the quantity of milk given by the average Indian cow during the lactation period. Large numbers of good cattle are issued year by year from the Government farms, and valuable bulls are made available to the agriculturists for breeding purposes. Notable results are, moreover, achieved at the Imperial Institute of Animal Industry at Bangalore, where dairy managers are given a practical training on modern lines. This institution also carries on the breeding of stock, and it has an animal nutrition section which conducts research into the question of the proper feeding of cattle. The Bangalore Institute has the advantage of possessing in its head, Mr. William Smith, an enthusiast of ability and energy, who has emphasised in his official reports the fact that the indigenous milk industry is mainly in the hands of men who are not only illiterate and steeped in what might be classed as "trade superstition," and has worked incessantly to provide a remedy for such a deplorable state of affairs.

The bare recital contained in this chapter is sufficient to show that the Agricultural Departments are doing a great work for India, and if as a result of the recommendations of the Linlithgow Commission, adequate financial resources are placed at their disposal, far greater advances will be possible. The Indian peasant, wedded as he is to social and religious customs which retard his economic progress, is ready to adopt new agricultural methods when it has been proved to him by practical demonstration that these methods will beyond all doubt increase his income. The work accomplished in this field by agricultural officers is worthy of the highest praise ; their patience, skill and devotion deserve both gratitude and admiration. Sir James Mackenna, a former Agricultural Adviser to the Government of India and a member of the Commission on Agriculture, once declared with truth that, if results of practical value were to be obtained, the agricultural officer must possess a thorough knowledge of Indian agriculture and a sympathetic feeling towards the people. "The cultivator," as he wrote, "is not concerned with the process of discovery. The concrete results of chemical, botanical and bacteriological research must be presented to him in a form which he can readily apply." The number of practical demonstrations carried out annually now runs into many thousands, and in addition hundreds of agricultural shows are arranged for the benefit of the cultivator. Cinema films have been used of late to supplement this class of work. Experiments have also been made with trains fitted up as travelling exhibitions, designed to bring home to the people the possibilities of improving their economic and physical well-being which may lie within their reach.

Although India is still backward in education, marked advance is being made. Critics who reproach the Government with the prevalence of illiteracy seldom show appreciation of the fact that the obstacles to be surmounted are unparalleled in any other country. It has been aptly said that the "tradition of education" is non-existent save among certain restricted castes or classes. Only in recent times, moreover, has it been grudgingly recognised that the education of females, who number 132 millions in British India, is desirable. Mr. J. A. Richey, formerly Educational Commissioner with the Government of India, in an address to the East India Association in November 1928, mentioned the decision of an important District Board to close all its girls' schools on the ground that female education was a waste of money. Another drawback is found in the bitter opposition of caste Hindus to the admission of the children of "untouchables" to educational institutions maintained by public funds. Divergences of language add to the difficulties to be surmounted; in the Province of Bihar and Orissa, for example, there are as many as six recognised vernaculars. Again, the rural classes who constitute the great bulk of the inhabitants of India, are only beginning to realise the value of education. The removal of village children from school before they derive any benefit from the instruction provided has been the cause of enormous waste of money and effort. In the end, the adoption of compulsion will, no doubt, prove a solution for this evil, but while Education Acts giving local bodies the option of adopting compulsory measures have been passed in the seven major Provinces, the results, on the whole, have been disappointing. Mr. Richey is of opinion that elementary education is now of such vital importance for the political, social and economic advancement of India that the responsibility for it should be assumed by Government instead of being left in the hands of municipalities and district boards. Still, the number of scholars in publicly recognised institutions is steadily increasing. Within ten years it has risen from some 7,350,000 to over 10,000,000, and the rate of advance is about half a million annually. The progress of the Punjab, in particular, is highly encouraging. Sir George Anderson, Director of Public Instruction in that Province, has shown that the number of pupils enrolled in the Punjab schools rose from

557,000 in 1920-21 to 1,198,000 in 1926-27, and he states that the marked increase in attendance at secondary schools, especially in backward areas, abundantly proves that many parents who are very poorly circumstanced are prepared to make any sacrifice so that their sons (but unfortunately not their daughters) shall receive the benefits of education. While the political leaders have done much in the Punjab Legislative Council by their speeches and by their support of educational demands, Sir George Anderson considers it probable that this movement has had its genesis in the people themselves, and has not been inspired from above. He further contends that among the causes of the progress recorded is the return of a large number of Punjabi soldiers from the War, men who, as he says, have seen life and the world, and are determined that their sons shall benefit by education. But, according to the same authority, while the political leaders have shown their readiness to vote financial grants for educational purposes, they still think that the needs of the beneficent Departments of Government can be met by a reduction in the police and in the work of general administration.

V

THE CONQUEST OF FAMINE

"The development of irrigation on a vast scale in the Punjab, and to a smaller extent elsewhere, has immensely increased the resources of the country; railways and roads have been extended, and the effects of the improvements both of internal and external communications have made themselves increasingly felt. It took India nearly a generation to re-act to the great changes in this respect which have been mentioned, but, since the commencement of the present century, the evidence of growing prosperity has been manifest to everyone whose acquaintance with India extends over the last twenty-five years."—*Report of the Royal Commission on Agriculture in India*, 1928.

THE conquest of famine is the greatest achievement of British administration in India. The task has been a long and an arduous one, and its results are in themselves an enduring monument to the men who participated in its accomplishment. India's crops depend in the main upon the monsoon rains, and the failure of the monsoon still means grievous loss to the cultivator. In the past it meant famine, grim and terrible, and the sufferings of the people were accentuated by deadly epidemic diseases. Famine at other times has been caused by floods; such is the irony of existence in India.

It is not difficult to realise that if the national industries of England or of the United States were completely paralysed for six months, grave hardships must inevitably ensue. In India the conditions formerly created by the failure of the crops were almost indescribable. The work of protecting a great agricultural population from the effects of famine thus engaged the anxious attention of generations of British officials. In the reports of successive Famine Commissions are to be found careful studies of the varied problems which from time to time presented themselves, and far-sighted recommendations directed towards the provision of effective remedies.

Apart from the direct methods of protecting India from famine which will presently be discussed, the development of the land revenue system under British rule has been of inestimable value in enhancing the ability of the cultivator to face periods of economic distress. The record of rights in land which followed an exhaustive enquiry, converted into a valuable possession property which the cultivator had hitherto found impossible to sell or to pledge when trouble came upon him. The record of rights provided the basis of the Government demand for land revenue, which is now the subject of periodical settlements (except in the permanently settled areas described further on), every effort being made by the settlement officers to avoid placing undue burdens on the people.

Under the ancient law of India the ruler is entitled to a certain proportion of the produce of the land unless he has limited or surrendered his rights in this respect. The resultant exactions of the State in pre-British days impoverished the cultivator. Extortionate demands made upon an industrious but helpless class perpetuated poverty and rendered it impossible for the agriculturist to make provision for the inevitable day when the crops would fail owing to the absence of rain. In its review of this phase of the agrarian problem, the Royal Commission on Agriculture points out that there were few periods in the recorded history of India prior to the advent of British administration when over extensive areas the internal peace was not greatly disturbed, and when the demands of the rulers on the land were not so heavy as to make its possession a liability rather than an asset. These demands were frequently arbitrary; they "varied with the needs of the time, the embarrassment of the ruler and the temperament and rapacity of the local authorities."

A revolution was effected by the preparation of a full record of the cultivator's rights in the land and the inauguration of a policy which ensured a just settlement of the extent of his liability for land revenue. It is unquestionable that the land revenue paid to-day inflicts no hardship on the people. From time to time the allegation is made that the charge is excessive, but this contention will not bear investigation, and is often palpably absurd. Sir Michael O'Dwyer, who possesses almost unique knowledge of the Punjab, has pointed out that when the British annexed that Province the selling value of land was five shillings per acre, or only double the heavy Sikh land tax. In 1926, he said, as a result of light assessment, the establishment of security and the construction of railways and irrigation works, the average selling price was more than three hundred times the British land tax, and stood at £33 per acre.

In 1902 the Government of India, in consequence of persistent attacks on their land revenue policy, published an exhaustive Resolution on the whole subject, in which they effectively disposed of the contention advanced by the late Mr. R. C. Dutt and others, that the intensity and frequency of famines had been largely due to the poverty created by over-assessment. This great State paper, drafted by Lord Curzon himself, was remarkable for its close reasoning and the obvious anxiety for the welfare of the cultivating class which inspired it. Fortified by the views of the Provincial Governments, the Government of

India examined in detail the arguments advanced by the critics, vindicated the general policy which had been pursued, and after laying down principles for imparting greater elasticity to assessment and collection, went on to show that the existing system was well suited to the conditions of the country, and more lenient in its incidence than at any previous period in its history. It was pointed out that in the Central Provinces alone successive droughts had during a period of seven years inflicted on the agricultural class losses estimated at upwards of forty crores of rupees, an amount equal to the land revenue for fifty years, while the State had expended in the relief of the distress in this area a sum equivalent to seven years' land revenue.

The critics of the Government's land revenue policy had put forward the remarkable theory that if the Permanent Settlement which still afflicts Bengal had been extended to other parts of the country, India would have been spared the "more dreadful and desolating famines we have witnessed in recent years." The crushing rejoinder contained in the Government of India's Resolution deserves more than passing notice, in view of the immunity from taxation which the landlords of that Province still enjoy. The Permanent Settlement of Bengal dates from the later period of the eighteenth century, when Lord Cornwallis made the grave blunder of effecting an arrangement by which the landholders were for all time to be subject to no enhancement of their payments to the State. Since that period the value of land in Bengal has undergone an enormous increase, but Government is unable to share in the enhancement, with the result that an unfair burden of taxation has to be borne by other industries. A horde of rent receivers, possessing no interest in the cultivator or in the progress of agriculture has, moreover, been brought into existence.

The Government of India had no difficulty in showing, first, that the cost of famine relief had been greater in Bengal than elsewhere, and that in place of being generously treated by the landlords, the Bengal cultivator was so persistently rackrented, impoverished and oppressed, that it had been necessary to pass a series of legislative measures for his protection. "It was not in fact in the Permanent Settlement of Bengal that the ryot has found his salvation," said the Resolution: "it has been in the laws which have been passed by the Supreme Government to check its licence and to moderate its abuses."

The truth is that the ability of the Indian cultivator to withstand famine is due entirely to the measures inaugurated and carried out under British administration. The record of rights in land, the introduction of periodical settlements of land revenue, the establishment of co-operative credit societies and the improvement of agricultural methods have all had their part in the work. But the most potent factors have been the construction of railways and the creation of the finest irrigation works in the world.

The Indian railway system comprises nearly 40,000 miles, and it is expected that within the next few years another 6,000 miles will have been added to this total, since a programme of extension is being steadily developed. More capital might with advantage have been expended in the past on railways, but the construction already completed has transformed the economic position. The cultivator need no longer grow sufficient produce to satisfy his own needs and no more; he has been placed within reach of markets, both in India and in countries beyond the seas, which offer him opportunities of profit and provide him with means of meeting with greater confidence a failure of the rains. An illustration of the advantages secured by the agriculturist from access to foreign markets is found in the fact that in the year 1927-28 the value of Indian merchandise exported, consisting to an overwhelming extent of the produce of the soil, was valued at 319 crores of rupees, or nearly £240,000,000.

The extension of railways has synchronized with the construction of great irrigation works, which have converted millions of acres of barren waste into fruitful fields. An official report on irrigation in India shows that on the average of the five years ending with 1925-26 nearly 12 per cent. of the entire cropped area of the country was irrigated by Government works, the annual value of the harvests raised on this area amounting to some £114,000,000, while the capital cost of the works was no more than £75,000,000. In the Punjab, the Land of the Five Rivers, where the facilities for irrigation are especially favourable, over two-fifths of the cropped area is now secure from the danger of drought, and only those who have seen mile after mile of golden wheat on what was once barren desert can realise the transformation that has taken place.

The famous Punjab Canal Colonies extend over 5,000,000 acres. In a single year the produce of this area has been valued at £20,000,000, of which £5,000,000 was estimated to be the profits of the cultivator. Mr. Darling, who has had long experience of the Punjab, has graphically depicted the territory which now constitutes the rich Montgomery Colony as it existed some fifteen years ago. It was then "a country of rolling sand dunes, patched with grass, and of hard unfruitful plains glistening with salt." To-day the Montgomery Colony is one of the richest rural areas in India, though here as elsewhere in the Punjab the cultivator has yet to be weaned from habits and customs which make rather for poverty than for prosperity. Sir Edward Maclagan, whose final years of service were spent as Governor of the Province, has described the Punjabi peasant as one of the finest and noblest of his kind. But unhappily it is only too true that " the tide of wealth that has been flowing into the Punjab for the last thirty or forty years continues to pass through the hands of the many, who have earned it by their toil, into the hands of the few, who acquire and retain it by their wit." There is evidence, however, that some, at least, of the 500,000 Punjabis who served in the Great War brought back with them, as the result of their observations among the agriculturists of France and Flanders, new ideas of life and of its material possibilities. It may be, then, that the time is not far distant when it will no longer be true to say that the profits of the moneylending class probably exceed those of all the cultivators of the Province combined, and when the sturdy peasant farmer will see the unwisdom of wasting his substance in the courts, to the enrichment of the legal fraternity and to his own impoverishment.

The work of the irrigation engineer is by no means at an end. Great projects are in hand, which, when completed, will materially increase Indian agricultural wealth. Foremost among these projects is the great Sukkur Barrage Scheme in Sind, which involves the construction of a barrage nearly a mile in length across the Indus, with sixty-six spans of sixty feet each. When this great work is completed the canals which will be fed with water will command an area of 7½ million acres, and will supply irrigation annually to 5½ million acres, or more than the entire cultivable area of Egypt. Three million acres of this land is now barren. Apart from increasing the agricultural production, it is expected that the inauguration of the scheme will lead to the cultivation of more valuable crops than are at present grown in Sind, including wheat and long staple cotton.

The Sutlej Valley project will provide perennial irrigation for two million acres, and also improve the water supply over an area of another three million acres. Other schemes contemplated in the Punjab are the Thal project, which, when carried out, will command an area of about a million and a half acres, partly in the desert districts of Mianwali and Mazaffargarh, and the Haveli project, which will bring perennial irrigation to some 700,000 acres.

In the United Provinces the Sarda Canal scheme is expected to irrigate annually nearly one million and three-quarter acres, while in the Madras Presidency there are several projects in hand or under consideration which will materially increase the agricultural output. It is estimated indeed that when all the works are completed the irrigated area in India will be no less than forty million acres.

A consideration which should not be overlooked is the direct benefit to the Indian taxpayer which has resulted from the construction of railways and irrigation works. At the end of the financial year 1927-28 the public debt of the country amounted in round figures to £743 millions, of which no less than £608 millions was represented by valuable revenue-producing assets. The total unproductive debt was £135 millions, or a little more than ten shillings per head of the population. What other country in the world can present such a favourable financial record ? In submitting his last Budget to the Indian Legislative Assembly Sir Basil Blackett was able to show what a great advance the credit of India had made in the London market since the War in relation to British Government and other gilt-edged securities. On April 30th, 1914, the Indian three per cent. loan was quoted at 75¼ ; on December 31st, 1927, it stood at 62¾. In the case of British Local Loans three per cent. stock the quotation was 87 in 1914 and 65 at the end of 1927, while London County Council three per cents. fell in the same period from 81 to 68¾. These figures are a striking testimony to the prudence and fidelity with which India's finances have been safeguarded. India, it has been said with truth, is the most lightly taxed country in the world. The incidence per head of population is, according to careful estimates, not more than nine shillings, even when the income-tax, which is not paid by the masses, is included in the computation. It is obvious that the lightness of this fiscal obligation is an important factor in enabling the people to withstand the evils arising from the failure of the crops.

The efficacy of the famine policy of the Administration has been put to the test on more than one occasion during the past quarter of a century. In the years 1907 and 1908 the whole of the United Provinces of Agra and Oudh, covering, with two small Indian States, an area of more than 112,000 square miles, with a population of 48,500,000, or considerably more than the total population of England and Wales, was affected more or less seriously by the failure of the monsoon rains. Yet at the close of the relief operations over 66,000 square miles of territory, carrying a population of nearly 30,000,000, Sir John Hewett, then Lieutenant-Governor, was able to state that "eleven deaths only or about a quarter of the number reported due to this cause in London last year could be attributed directly to want of food. There was no inclination to conceal deaths due to starvation, and the fact that so few deaths occurred is an eloquent testimony to the adequacy of the relief measures." A marked change was witnessed in the attitude of the people when compared with the experience of earlier famines. The cultivators had formerly shown despondency when faced with a great calamity; they now worked vigorously in the sowing of new crops, and expressed gratitude to Government and its officers for providing them with funds to assist them in the task of repairing their losses. The labours of civil officials, British and Indian, were magnificent, and Sir John Hewett paid a high tribute to the courage and devotion of Indian subordinates, who throughout an epidemic of cholera, caused in the famine area by pilgrims, kept to their posts at the risk and in some cases at the cost of their lives. The conduct of military officers on famine duty was also the subject of eulogy. The work entrusted to them was often carried out under most trying climatic conditions; they remained in camps, frequently in tents, throughout the hot weather, and they displayed the utmost tact and courtesy in their dealings with the people.

The assistance given to the Administration by non-official helpers was a gratifying feature of the work of relief. "Those on whose behalf the work was undertaken," wrote the Lieutenant-Governor, "are reported on all sides to be most grateful to the Government for the help that has been given to them. The expression of this feeling has been probably more articulate than on previous occasions, and opinion is unanimous that they are not only grateful but also contented. There is every hope that the effects of the affliction through which they have passed will be only evanescent. The general verdict is that the trial through which the Province has just passed has served to bring all classes into closer sympathy with each other and with the Government."

In 1918-19 a failure of the monsoon which affected a much larger area was experienced; indeed, not a single Province escaped the evils attendant on the failure of the rains. The situation was exceptionally unfavourable, owing to the great rise in prices both of food and clothing which had been experienced, largely arising from the world disturbance created by the Great War. It was estimated that the loss in food production resulting from the failure of the monsoon was at least 20,000,000 tons, and the Government of India were confronted with difficulties of the gravest character. In addition to adopting measures to regulate or prohibit the export of foodstuffs, the authorities imported 200,000 tons of wheat from Australia. This action helped to reassure the public and it tended to check the advance in wheat prices. In view of the abnormal dearness of clothing, the Government of India also arranged for the manufacture of standardized cotton cloth, 22,000,000 yards of which were distributed among the various Provinces. The failure of the rains combined with the high prices of the necessaries of life inflicted great hardship on the poor. But the measures adopted by Government, including liberal loans to the cultivating classes and the opening of shops at which cheap grain could be procured, were sufficient to deal with the distress, and even in districts where prices ruled highest, the people withstood the strain in a manner which caused surprise even to those who realised the economic advance India had made during the present century. In fact, the maximum number of persons on relief was not one-tenth of the number relieved in the famine of 1900, when the crop failure was at least as severe as that of 1918-19.

India must continue to depend on the fitful monsoon for the greater part of her harvests, but when the rains fail the situation can be faced with confidence so long as Government is able to step in with measures of relief. Considering the grave obligations which devolve on the authorities when the crops perish for want of water, it is a serious reflection that men who pay lip service to the cause of the people should preach the doctrine of non-co-operation with the "bureaucracy." For there is every reason to fear that if serious dislocation of the machinery of administration synchronized with a failure of the rains the Indian peasantry would be involved in a catastrophe unparalleled in modern times.

VI

THE WORK OF CHRISTIAN MISSIONS

THE value of the services rendered to India by British administration is more widely recognised than the work of Christian missions in that country. Inspired by the high ideals of their Master, thousands of men and women have gone out to the East from Western countries and devoted their lives to the greatest task open to humanity. The popular belief that the missionary confines his efforts to proselytising among the adherents of religions other than his own is scarcely flattering to the intelligence of those who hold it. More impressive, indeed, than the preaching of the Gospel in India is the manner in which the teachings of the Founder of the Christian faith are applied by the mission workers.

The striking increase in the number of Indian Christians in recent years is mainly due to the welcome accorded by outcastes to a creed which proclaims the Fatherhood of God and the brotherhood of man. At the census of 1921 the actual number of Christians was returned at 4,753,000, an increase of 879,000 over the figures of 1911, and of these 93 out of each 100 were Indians. There were, according to the Census Commissioner, two and a half times as many Christians in India in 1921 as there were forty years earlier. But apart from securing actual converts, the missions have created among the educated classes spiritual interest in the teachings of Christ, which is admirably discussed in Dr. Stanley Jones's *Christ of the Indian Road.* Dr. Jones, after referring to the mass movement of the outcastes towards Christianity, points out that there is a more remarkable movement at the other end of society. "Do not misunderstand me," he adds, "they are not knocking at the doors for baptism, nor are they enamoured of our ecclesiastical systems or our civilisation, but there is an amazing turn in thought towards Christ." It is unquestionable, moreover, that the social welfare movements inaugurated in recent years by both Mahomedans and Hindus have largely received their inspiration from the example provided by Christian missions.

The epic of mission work in India has yet to be written; it is only possible here to touch briefly on what has been and is being accomplished by a few of the innumerable societies whose institutions are spread throughout the country, from the North-West Frontier to Assam and from Baluchistan to Southern India. No

Western church of any note has failed to take its part in the work. British missions predominate, but the United States has a worthy share.

A glance at the activities of these Christian bodies is sufficient to indicate the nature of their services to India. Their schools provide education for hundreds of thousands of pupils; their hospitals bring medical relief to millions in the course of each year. Homes for women, orphan asylums, leper asylums, agricultural settlements and co-operative societies are conducted with success; members of degraded criminal tribes have been converted into self-respecting and industrious men and women.

It may seem invidious to name a few individual societies, but it would require a volume to do justice to them all. Among the outcastes results have been achieved which are little short of miraculous. The operations of the Church Missionary Society, for instance, cover an enormous field. Its schools and colleges in India number 2,386, and are attended by nearly 100,000 pupils. Among the untouchables of Southern India work has been carried on by the Society for many years; it has indeed as many as 1,118 schools in the Telegu country, which educate 24,000 children, mostly of the depressed classes. In medical relief the Society has mainly concentrated on Kashmir and on the North-West Frontier, where the heroic Pennell, whose name will long be held in grateful remembrance by the tribesmen, laboured and died.

In all, the Church Missionary Society has ten major and four branch hospitals in India. The records of the Afghan Medical Mission, which it founded at Peshawar, give some idea of the regard in which human life is held in that region. Afghans, Afridis, Mohmands, Swatis, are among the varied races who come to the hospitals for treatment, many of them to be healed of bullet wounds received at the hands of their enemies in the fierce blood feuds which are waged among the tribesmen. Cataract is a sore scourge on the Frontier. Dr. Bolton, writing from Bannu, says there are two cataract seasons—in spring and early autumn, when the air is most free from dust, and he adds: "It is wonderful how the people from the distant villages know of these times, and a little stream of blind old women will come down led by a husband, or even a child, 'to have their curtain removed.'"

At Shikarpur, in Sind, a hospital is opened for six weeks in the year, and Dr. Holland, who is in charge of the Society's Quetta hospital, goes to Shikarpur during this period, largely for the purpose of ophthalmic work. Between January 1st and February 20th, 1928, as many as 3,000 operations were performed, and as a rule about half of the total cases dealt with surgically here are for cataract.

Few of the fortunate people who have visited Kashmir have failed to hear of the work of Dr. Neve and the Rev. C. E. Tyndale-Biscoe for the Kashmiris, which in its broad scope and vision has achieved memorable results. The Church Missionary Society's hospital at Srinagar is highly valued by the people, and in the domain of education and medicine alike, the moral and physical benefits conferred by the missionaries on the rising generation have aroused the admiration of all serious-minded visitors to this beautiful land.

Among other institutions for which the Church Missionary Society is responsible is an orphanage for boys at Sikandra, near Agra, which was founded after the famine of 1837 for the rescue of children who were left derelict owing to that visitation. Here Indian boys are not only given the usual school education, but are taught trades, so that they may take their share in the business of life. A high standard of conduct is set before them; provision is made for team games, and they are afforded opportunities which they never could have hoped for but for the presence of the Mission.

A C.M.S. settlement near Benares is devoted to the education and training of Indian girls. The idea of family life dominates the whole scheme of the settlement; groups of six to eight children compose each family, and a senior girl is appointed as "mother." The children here are thoroughly trained as housewives, and when they reach a suitable age for marriage they start life fully equipped for the duties that lie before them.

Another important organisation, the London Missionary Society, which is active in Bengal and in certain areas in South India, has, in addition to its hospitals, 850 schools of all grades, in which over 31,000 boys and 16,400 girls receive education. Its medical institutions number 20, including hospitals with 506 beds, which give treatment to 9,000 in-patients and nearly 200,000 out-patients yearly. The modest records of its achievements are full of inspiration and hope.

It has more than once been emphasised by eminent British officials that the aboriginals of Chota Nagpur are deeply indebted to the Belgian Jesuit missionaries who have laboured among them. In the domain of education and co-operation the work of the Fathers has been, and is, of a marvellous character, considering that they found the people steeped in ignorance, and, too often, crushed by the oppression of landlords and the exactions of usurers. Not only have the missionaries founded over 700 schools, culminating in the St. John's High School at Ranchi, but they have established a co-operative credit bank, with nearly 1,500 village branches, the managing staff of which is formed entirely of aboriginals.

The pioneer of the present mission was Father Constantine Lievens, a man of great ability, who studied the language of the tribes, and made himself acquainted with the conditions of the local land tenure, and was thus able to protect the people from the rapacity of the landlords and to secure them justice in the courts.

An eminent member of the Indian Educational Service once expressed to me his unbounded admiration of the devotion of the Fathers, some of them men of high attainments, who might have distinguished themselves in any walk of life. They worked among the people in the fields, he said, stood by them when they were unjustly prosecuted, administered to them in sickness, and brought them comfort and hope in the hour of death. An inspiring account of the Mission given by Father Van der Schueren, in an address to the East India Association, is worthy of study by anyone who is interested in the backward races of India.

The confidence of the people in the Belgian missionaries was illustrated in a remarkable manner during the Great War. The Government, desirous of recruiting labour for work on the Western Front, approached the Mission authorities in order to obtain their support. The response, Father Van der Schueren says, was excellent, but all who volunteered insisted on the condition that they should be accompanied by

Fathers, who should be in charge of them throughout. The Government agreed, and nearly 4,000 men were enrolled who proceeded to the Front in the care of two Fathers of the Mission, where they rendered an excellent account of themselves.

Fundamental differences may exist between the doctrines of the Jesuit Fathers of Chota Nagpur and the tenets of the Welsh Calvinistic Methodists whose field of labour lies among the tribes of the Assam Hills. Yet in its essence the work of both is the same; both are inspired by Christian devotion and both have achieved results that justify their faith. Observers who have visited Assam have been impressed by the contrast between the bright and well-kept houses of the Christian hillmen and the surroundings of their animist neighbours. Mr. B. C. Allen, who, as a Civil Servant, occupied the position of Commissioner of the Assam Valley Division, has indeed described the Christian Khasis as the cleanest, the most prosperous, the best educated, and the most reliable of their tribe. Welshmen passing through the Khasi country have been astonished to hear the old Welsh hymn tunes, familiar in the chapels of their native land, sung with fervour by the primitive hill people, converts of the Welsh Calvinists, who were the pioneers of Christian effort in this remote region of the world.

Missionary work among the criminal tribes of India has been attended with exceptional difficulties, for the problem presented is unique and perplexing. These Ishmaels of society regard robbery as a legitimate not to say a laudable occupation; they glory in successful raids on the property of others. Many of the tribes wander about the country in pursuit of their nefarious calling, and the efforts of the police to keep them within check are rendered nugatory by the largeness of their numbers and their vagrant propensities. In his interesting book, *Crime in India*, the late Mr. S. M. Edwardes, who had wide experience of police administration, pointed out that spontaneous efforts at reform by some of the tribes were rendered ineffectual by the hostile attitude of the upper classes. Where they attempted to send their children to schools, schoolmasters resented and actively discouraged the entrance of children of criminal tribes. Two boys of this class, who were sent to a school of carpentry by a local official, were so grievously persecuted that they were compelled to leave, and an official report stated that such hatred and opposition on the part of the higher castes were met with everywhere and had proved an almost insuperable obstacle to the moral and social improvement of the criminal tribes.

No more unpromising material for reformation could perhaps be found than these degraded outcastes, yet it has been amply proved that they are capable of higher things. In some Provinces Governments have attempted to grapple with the problem, but the most promising efforts towards its solution have been contributed by the Salvation Army, which has on many occasions been publicly thanked for its labours. The operations of the Army in this field were inaugurated in the United Provinces during Sir John Hewett's term of office as Lieutenant-Governor, and Sir John himself expressed the belief in a Government Resolution, that the Army's efforts showed the way to the solution of a hitherto unsolved problem. More recently, Lord Ronaldshay, after visiting a silk factory conducted by the Salvation Army, in which young members of criminal tribes were working, warmly eulogised the Army's activities; and it is beyond question that its work has resulted in transforming former "hopeless enemies of mankind" into useful and industrious citizens. After his retirement from India Sir John Hewett, in a speech in London, said he was convinced that in time the Salvation Army would succeed in the object it had in view—namely, the absorption of the criminal tribes into the ordinary population. When that had been done Commissioner Booth Tucker and those who worked with him would have combined to achieve one of the greatest moral reformations the world had ever seen.

Nor must the services rendered to the Doms of Benares by the Wesleyan Methodist Missionary Society be overlooked in even a brief recital of the work done among criminal tribes. *Prisoners Released*, written by the Rev. C. Phillips Cape, who gave some ten years of his life to the Doms, is one of the most fascinating of the books on missionary effort in India. Sir Herbert Risley, in discussing the origin of the Doms, states that for centuries past they have been condemned to the most menial duties and have served as the helots of the entire Hindu community, and save to men of unwavering faith and tireless devotion the task of weaning them from their vices must seem a hopeless one. Yet it has been steadily pursued, and Dr. Robert F. Horton declared that no memory stood out more vividly of things he saw in India than that of his visit to the Doms. Clearest of all was the picture of a Brahmin convert, who stood there with these untouchables —the Brahman evangelist—representative of the highest caste in India; the Doms—the "outcastes of the outcastes."

The success achieved in bringing relief to the victims of leprosy forms one of the brightest and most inspiring chapters in the history of Christian mission work in India. It is impossible to ascertain with exactitude the number of lepers in the country. The census figures relating to this subject are not to be relied upon, but Dr.

Muir, the Leprosy Worker at the Calcutta School of Tropical Medicine, states that recent figures obtained from a carefully conducted but limited survey tend to confirm the computation that there are between half a million and one million lepers in India. Until relief came from the far-off countries, this "Army of Sorrow" had no hope of succour or of cure. To-day, through the efforts of the Mission to Lepers, there are 52 leper asylums and homes for untainted children of lepers, with over 7,000 inmates, managed or aided by the Mission. In the great majority of cases the superintendents of these institutions are mission workers, who give their services without monetary reward.

Lepers of all castes and creeds are admitted to the asylums; there is no compulsion whatever in religious matters. The gratitude of these unhappy people for the care bestowed upon them is pathetic to witness, and, thanks to the scientific work of Sir Leonard Rogers and Dr. Muir, it is possible to hold out definite hope of cure to lepers who are prepared to submit themselves for treatment. Dr. Muir is now able to make the definite statement that "given ordinarily favourable circumstances, a patient determined to get better, and a doctor who understands his work and is willing to take trouble, there are few cases in which all active signs of leprosy cannot be stamped out."

The disease of leprosy has been known in India from time immemorial. It is mentioned in the Vedas, more than 1,000 years before the Christian era. If ever it should be entirely eliminated, the deliverance of India from this scourge will be due to the pity evoked among men and women in distant countries by the sufferings of its victims.

Within the past year or two the condition of the women of India has been the subject of considerable discussion both in England and the United States. A very large proportion of the female population of the country are secluded under the purdah system, a mode of life which is unhygienic, mentally inhibiting and wholly inconsistent with progress. The effects of the purdah system open up a wide field for service to the women doctors of the missions. The work of these doctors in the zenanas is valued beyond measure, and in addition to providing skilled treatment for the sick, they exercise a salutary influence by establishing purdah schools for children.

Mission hospitals have also proved a valuable boon to Indian women. The St. Stephen's Hospital at Delhi, carried on by the Cambridge Mission with the support of the Society for the Propagation of the Gospel, and one of the largest of its kind in India, is entirely staffed by women, among whom are European and Indian doctors and sisters, and Indian nurses and dispensers. A training school for nurses, dispensers and *dais* (indigenous midwives), forms part of the work. The training of *dais* in hygienic methods is of supreme importance, since the practices followed by untrained women of this class are so horrible that it seems almost miraculous that any mother or infant survives treatment at their hands. The Society for the Propagation of the Gospel, it should be stated, assists a large number of hospitals and dispensaries in India.

It may seem invidious, as I have already indicated, to omit from this brief survey any reference to the labours of other missionary bodies in India. But it is not possible in a single chapter to give them their due. There exists in the reports of the societies, however, a wealth of valuable information, which is readily accessible to anyone who desires to gain knowledge of Christian work and achievement among the diverse races of the Indian continent. The name of William Carey conjures up in the mind the linguistic achievements of this gifted man; the famous College at Serampore remains as a living monument of his labours in Bengal. The Baptist Missionary Society with which he was associated was a pioneer among the modern missionary bodies entering the Indian field, and its territory includes Bihar and the United Provinces as well as Bengal. Scotland, again, may contemplate with pride the work of Alexander Duff, and the Scottish Mission Colleges in Calcutta, Madras and Bombay testify to the interest in India of a country which is famous for its devotion to the cause of education. In the same sphere of activity the United States occupies an honoured place, the American Mission Colleges at Lahore and Allahabad being prominent among India's institutions for higher education. The Mission presses have contributed to the cause of education by their translations of noted books into the vernaculars and by disseminating the literary products of eminent Western writers throughout India.

It must be admitted that bare statistics present an arid appearance. But no one with a spice of imagination can fail to realise in some degree the wealth of devotion, on the one hand, and the untold benefits, on the other, suggested by the collected figures published in the *Directory of Christian Missions in India.* Nearly 100 agricultural settlements, over 100 co-operative banks and societies, 220 hospitals, 190 dispensaries, 68 leper institutions, 143 orphanages, 65 homes for women, 178 industrial schools and thousands of primary schools—these are among the contributions of "Western materialism" towards the welfare of India.

VII

"PASSIVE RESISTANCE" AND REBELLION

> "The children born of thee are sword and fire,
> Red ruin and the breaking up of laws."
>
> *Tennyson* ("*Guinevere*").

IT cannot seriously be denied that marked progress in general prosperity has been made by India during the past quarter of a century. The factors which have contributed to that result have already been enumerated. With the co-operation of Indians employed in the public Services and of others who are animated by a sincere and intelligent desire for the advancement of their country, Government has been able to pursue with success the task of raising the economic status of the people, of safeguarding the masses from the dangers of famine and of providing them with educational facilities.

It is equally true that these efforts have been checked and hampered by insensate agitations, culminating in grave disorders, the destruction of property and the loss of thousands of lives. The Indian people are naturally law-abiding. But in India, as in other countries, there are dangerous elements, which lend a ready ear to appeals to their cupidity or to their fanaticism. These elements have on many occasions been worked upon so successfully by men professing to have the good of India at heart that they have resorted to terrible excesses and threatened the peace of the whole country. The Punjab rising, as we shall see, was caused by the dissemination of shameless mendacities among the people, many of whom were induced to accept as gospel the assertion that Government was about to inaugurate a policy of intolerable oppression and wholesale confiscation.

The history of the outbreaks which followed the passing of what were known as the Rowlatt Acts throws lurid light on the methods and designs of the politicians who were concerned in the agitation against these measures. Towards the close of the year 1917 the Government of India, with the approval of the Secretary of State, appointed a Committee to investigate and report on the nature and extent of the criminal conspiracies connected with the revolutionary movement in India and to advise as to the legislation that might be necessary to enable the Government to deal effectively with the conspirators. The President of the Committee was Mr. Justice Rowlatt of the King's Bench Division, the other members being Sir Basil Scott, Chief Justice of Bombay, Dewan Bahadur C. V. Kumaraswami Sastri, Judge of the High Court of Madras, Sir

Verney Lovett, an eminent member of the Indian Civil Service, and Mr. Provash Chandra Mitter, vakil of the Calcutta High Court. The Committee was thus preponderatingly judicial in its character, and it included two Indian lawyers of high standing and repute.

During the Great War it had been found possible by means of the Defence of India Act to impose some check on the activities of the leaders of the revolutionary movement, which had its focus in Bengal. The special legislation enacted during the War would, however, lapse soon after the declaration of peace; the persons interned under the Defence of India Act would be due for release, and, at the same time, the terms of imprisonment of many dangerous convicts would be coming to an end. After an exhaustive examination of the evidence, the Committee arrived at the unanimous conclusion that the Government should be armed with new powers against the revolutionaries, and they formulated the proposals on which the Rowlatt Bills were subsequently based.

The evidence laid before the Committee disclosed a grave condition of affairs. It showed that the anarchist conspiracy had its origin in the agitations set on foot in Bengal after the introduction by Lord Curzon of a Bill for the reform of the Indian Universities and his decision, on administrative grounds, to effect what is known as the Partition of Bengal. The latter step was decided upon owing to the unwieldy character of the Province, which had an area of 189,000 square miles and a population of 78 millions. Sir Andrew Fraser, the Lieutenant-Governor, stated at the time that, owing to the great area and enormous population of the Province, it had become practically impossible to conduct the administration efficiently, and the Eastern districts notoriously suffered from neglect.

The revolutionaries took full advantage of the opportunities presented to them. The agitation set on foot had led to an attempted boycott of British goods, in the enforcement of which boys of the *bhadralok*, or educated class, participated with hysterical fervour. It was to boys and young students, therefore, that the revolutionaries addressed their efforts. The necessity of collecting bombs and arms for the purpose of ejecting the British from India was openly preached; and an eminent Indian judge declared from the Bench that the revolutionary literature disseminated "does suggest that such principles as the religious principle of absolute surrender to the Divine Will, a doctrine common to many religions, are employed by designing and unscrupulous men to influence and unbalance weak-minded persons and thus ultimately bend them to become instruments in the commission of nefarious crimes from which they might otherwise recoil with horror." It was urged by the leaders of the movement that soldiers must be seduced from their allegiance; that "political dacoity" was justifiable, because it was "for the good of society"; that an organisation must be created which "would develop its inspiration by the murder of officials." After reviewing the propaganda and methods of the revolutionary organisation, the Rowlatt Committee proceeded to trace "a gradual development of a series of wilfully calculated crimes, of bomb outrages, of dacoities committed against helpless people in far-away villages, of secret murders, of assassinations of Indian police officers, whose only fault was their courageous and undeviating loyalty." The reader who desires to study this subject in detail will find all the necessary materials in the report of the Rowlatt Committee.

It may be said here that the record of barbarities committed, often by immature youths of good family, seemed almost incredible; that the conspirators entered into relations with German agents for the landing of arms in Bengal during the War, and that the terrorisation and murder of witnesses constituted a potent weapon for the evasion of punishment. The recruitment of revolutionaries among schoolboys, moreover, was carried on with assiduity, and two headmasters who endeavoured to check these sinister proceedings were mercilessly assassinated.

Although the centre of the movement was Bengal, revolutionary plots were set on foot in other Provinces by Bengali emissaries; while in the Punjab there arose the dangerous Sikh Ghadr conspiracy, which had rebellion as its object, led to many outrages and "came within an ace of causing widespread bloodshed." This movement was participated in mainly by Sikhs who had returned from America, where they had fallen under the influence of notorious seditionists. It is gratifying, however, to have the testimony of Sir Michael O'Dwyer that the Sikh community as a body helped the Government throughout in the struggle with these denationalised Sikhs, who in America had renounced many of the essential Sikh practices and were now bringing disgrace on the Sikh name. Through the agency of the Defence of India Act, the Punjab Government found itself able to restore order. The Special Tribunals constituted under the Act dealt fearlessly with the conspirators, 136 of whom were found guilty of offences, nearly all of which were punishable with death. The number actually hanged was twenty.

The Rowlatt Committee found that very few Mahomedans were concerned in the conspiracies which have been described. But in August, 1916, the plot known as the "Silk Letters" case was discovered. This plot aimed at overthrowing

British rule by an attack on the North-West Frontier, supplemented by a Mahomedan rising in India. The promoters of the plot succeeded in getting into touch with the Germans, and a special mission was despatched from Berlin to Afghanistan in pursuance of the conspirators' designs. The mission proved a failure, but the Indian leaders involved remained in Afghanistan, whence, describing themselves as the "Provisional Government of India," they despatched letters to the Governor of Russian Turkestan and to the then Tsar, inviting Russia to co-operate in overthrowing British rule. The "Provisional Government" also proposed to form an alliance with Turkey, and with this end in view attempted to send letters to one Mahmud Hassan at Mecca, referring to the projected formation of an "Army of God," which was to obtain recruits in India and to effect an alliance among Islamic rulers. These letters, which were written on yellow silk, fell into British hands, as also did Mahmud Hassan and four of his companions, who were interned as prisoners of war. Mr. Justice Rowlatt and his colleagues were convinced by the evidence placed at their disposal of the anxiety of a number of Mahomedan fanatics to provoke first sedition and then rebellion in India, the methods of these men ranging from subterranean intrigue and propaganda to open defection. Against their designs, said the Rowlatt Committee, "the loyalty of the general Moslem community and the effective power of the Government are the only safeguards."

The Rowlatt Committee reported that in the absence of special powers outside the ordinary law, the difficulties of grappling with the conspiracies would have been grave indeed. They cited the statement of the Calcutta High Court that many assassinations, murders and bomb-throwing outrages had taken place, and that the victims generally had been persons assisting Crown prosecutions. Again, in a memorandum supplied to the Committee, a Bengali lawyer of experience stated: "I have myself noticed that in several cases the witnesses have been seized with trembling when they went up to the dock to identify the accused persons." Further, the Committee pointed out that since the year 1906 revolutionary outrages in Bengal had numbered 210 and attempts at committing such outrages had amounted to 101. Definite information was in the hands of the police of the complicity of no less than 1,038 persons in these offences. But only 84 had been convicted of specified crimes, 30 of whom were tried by tribunals constituted under the Defence of India Act. From January 1st, 1915, to June 30th, 1916, there were 14 murders, eight of them being of police officers, for which it had not been possible to place anyone on trial.

The Committee accordingly put forward recommendations to enable Government to secure the conviction and punishment of offenders and to check the spread of conspiracy and the commission of crimes. Two Bills based on these recommendations were introduced by the Government of India in the old Legislative Council in 1919. The first of the two measures was intended to make it possible for persons accused of anarchical crimes to be tried by a court consisting of three High Court Judges, with no right of appeal. The procedure, however, was to be brought into operation only when the Governor-General was satisfied that crime of this character was prevalent in a particular area. Further, Local Governments were to be empowered to order persons whom they believed to be active participants in revolutionary movements to furnish security or to reside in a specified place. As a precaution against any abuse of these powers, a safeguard was provided in the form of an investigating authority, which was to include a judicial officer and a non-official Indian, who were to examine the material upon which orders against any persons were based. When the Governor-General was convinced that the public safety was threatened, Local Governments were to be empowered to arrest persons reasonably believed to be implicated in the offences which were being committed and to confine them in such places as were prescribed. A number of persons were already detained, and the Committee emphasised that it was impossible to contemplate their automatic release on the expiry of the Defence of India Act six months after the War. One man recently arrested was undoubtedly guilty of four murders and had been concerned in 18 dacoities, of which five had involved further murders.

The second Rowlatt Bill provided for a permanent change in the criminal law. Any person found in possession of a seditious document with the intention of publishing or circulating it was to be liable to imprisonment, and it was to be made permissible to promise official protection against violence to an accused person willing to turn King's evidence. Magistrates, again, were to have power to direct a preliminary enquiry by the police in the case of certain offences in regard to which, under the existing law, a prosecution could not be instituted without the authorisation of a Local Government.

This brief exposition of the nature of the two Bills is necessary to render it possible to realise the true inwardness of the upheaval which followed their passing into law. The debates on the measures in the Legislative Council, at which I was present, were of an astonishing character. In vain did members of the Government of India assure the Council that the legislation would be directed against revolutionary crime alone; in vain did the Home Member, Sir William Vincent, produce intercepted correspondence showing that seditionists still at large were waiting for the release of the "old workers" confined under the Defence of India Act, to recommence their activities, which included looting, arson, dacoity and murder. The criminals against whom the legislation was directed, said Sir William Vincent, were "enemies of civilisation, enemies of progress, and enemies of any form of organised Government, whether European or Indian."

An atmosphere of unreality and make-believe pervaded the discussions on the Bills. One member declared that everyone whose opinion was worth having seemed to believe that "if this Bill is passed into law untold misery will be brought into this land"; another declaimed: "You may enlarge your Councils, you may devise wide electorates, but the men who will then fill your Councils will be toadies, timid men, and the bureaucracy, armed with these repressive powers, will reign unchecked under the outward forms of a democratic Government." An agitation set on foot in the country was characterised by similar banalities. One orator predicted that when the Bills became law, "life will be impossible for a single day." Another affirmed that the measures "would divide husband from wife, tear away innocent children from the bosom of the father, would break the ties of friendship and extinguish the flame of love." Yet the proposed legislation was intended to supersede far more drastic measures already in operation, which had been in force for several years.

The intervention of Mr. Gandhi gave a stimulus to the agitation against the Bills. That gentleman asserted that the Rowlatt Committee had "utterly ignored the historical fact that the millions in India are by nature the gentlest on earth." He also issued a pledge by which those who took it affirmed that if the Bills were passed they would "refuse civilly to obey these laws" and "such other laws as a committee to be hereafter appointed may think fit." They further affirmed that they would "faithfully follow truth and refrain from violence to life, person or property."

The Bills were duly passed, and the firstfruits of Mr. Gandhi's *Satyagraha,* or "passive resistance," movement were soon forthcoming. So far from being conducted on peaceful lines, the agitation developed into rioting and bloodshed, and in the Punjab into open rebellion.

At Ahmedabad, in the Bombay Presidency, the mob committed acts of incendiarism and violence. Attacks were made upon non-official Europeans and upon British and Indian officers. A European sergeant of police was dragged out of a shop and murdered. The walls of a police station were defaced by revolutionary inscriptions such as: "The British Raj is gone: the King of England is defeated and Swaraj is established," and "Kill all Europeans: murder them wherever they are found." At Viramgam in the Ahmedabad district, attacks were made on the railway and on Government offices; an Indian magistrate, Mr. Madhavlal, was dragged from a friend's house into the road by the rioters, who drenched his clothing with paraffin oil and set fire to him while he was still alive. They then heaped Government records on his burning body, which was completely consumed.

In Delhi serious riots also occurred, but the gravest outbreaks of all were witnessed in the Punjab, which resulted in a terrible record of bloodshed and destruction. The allegation that the troubles had their origin in public indignation against the Rowlatt Acts is pure fiction. An honest exposition of the provisions of these measures would have made no impression whatever upon the people. A campaign of unrestrained mendacity was accordingly launched in order to inflame the passions of the populace. The Punjab villagers were assured that under the Rowlatt Acts if two or three people were seen talking together they would be arrested by the police; that no man would be able to marry without obtaining Government sanction and paying a fee to the authorities; that if a person died a tax must be paid to Government before the body could be disposed of. Another lie well calculated to arouse intense feeling among peasant cultivators was to the effect that the crops were the property of Government who could seize them whenever they thought fit. It was these mendacities and not the provisions of the Rowlatt Act which created violent and widespread hostility to the Government among people who had no concern with politics or ordinary political agitation.

Barbarous murders of Europeans at Amritsar and elsewhere, attacks on railways and telegraphic communications, incendiarism and looting created alarm and indignation among the more reasonable of the politicians who had opposed the Rowlatt legislation. At Amritsar the European manager and assistant manager of the National Bank of India were beaten to death by the mob, and their bodies burnt in a pile of bank furniture. A like fate befell the European manager of the Alliance Bank, and a lady missionary was brutally beaten and left for dead in the street.

The declaration of martial law and the vigorous measures adopted by Sir Michael O'Dwyer and the military authorities were successful in suppressing the rebellion, but not until hundreds of lives had been lost and immense damage done to property.

These terrible events led Mrs. Besant, who had opposed the Rowlatt legislation, to declare that: "The cutting of telegraph wires, the derailment of troop trains, the burning of railway stations, the setting free of jail birds are not the action of *Satyagrahis* nor even of casual rioters, but of revolutionaries."

After the trouble had subsided a demand for an enquiry into alleged "excesses" by the authorities in the course of suppressing the rebellion was raised. The Government of India accordingly appointed a committee, under the presidency of Lord Hunter, whose report led to the censure of the late General Dyer for having, as it was contended, continued firing longer than was necessary on the mob gathered in the Jalianwala Bagh at Amritsar, when between 300 and 400 persons were killed. It was maintained, on the one hand, that General Dyer's action had saved the Punjab; on the other, it was alleged that he had been guilty of callous cruelty. It is not necessary to reopen this discussion, but it may be recalled that in his address to the jury, after the protracted proceedings in the trial of the libel action brought in London by Sir Michael O'Dwyer against Sir Sankaran Nair, Mr. Justice McCardie expressed his entire disagreement with the Hunter Committee's decision in these words: "Subject to your judgment, speaking with full deliberation and knowing the whole of the evidence given in this case, I express my view that General Dyer, in the grave and exceptional circumstances acted rightly, and, in my opinion, upon the evidence, he was wrongly punished by the Secretary of State for India. That is my view, and I need scarcely say that I have weighed every circumstance, every new detail that was not before the Hunter Committee. . . ."

The insensate agitation which had been set on foot in connection with the Rowlatt Acts not only caused great loss of life in India but was destined to bring about an attempted invasion by Amanullah, then Amir of Afghanistan. The Amir had issued a letter denouncing the Rowlatt legislation, which was circulated both in his own country and in India. His proceedings were described in a proclamation by Lord Chelmsford, as Viceroy and Governor-General. The Amir, said Lord Chelmsford, had professed to his people that in India neither men's property nor their religion was safe; that three men were forbidden to speak together; that Moslems were excluded from their mosques and Hindus from their temples. Relying on these false statements, the Afghan ruler called on Moslems and Hindus alike to show him allegiance. He was also responsible for the assertion that Sikhs had fired on British troops; that Germany was about to renew the War and that the English had been destroyed.

Inspired by the hope that British subjects would be seduced from their allegiance by his blandishments, the Amir launched military operations against India. The situation was unquestionably grave, but the Army in India, British and Indian alike, responded magnificently to the demands made upon them. There were at that time in India a number of British regiments which, after long and arduous service in the Great War, were awaiting demobilisation. But many of these brave men never saw their homes and their families again; they died in the grim and arid mountain regions of the North-West Frontier. Large numbers of Indian troops who had proceeded to their homes on leave were also recalled for service, and some idea of the magnitude of the operations against the Afghans and their tribal allies may be gathered from the statement of Sir Charles Monro, Commander-in-Chief in India, that at one stage the strength of the force employed trans-Indus consisted of 340,000 men. The campaign was conducted under appalling climatic conditions, a heat wave of abnormal severity occurring over the whole of the North-West Frontier Province and the Punjab shortly after the outbreak of hostilities. An epidemic of cholera of exceptional virulence among the civil population added to the difficulties of the campaign. The disease spread to the troops and caused serious apprehension until it was stamped out by the efforts of the Medical Service.

In describing the events of the third Afghan War of 1919, Sir Charles Monro paid a high tribute to the cheerfulness and fine military spirit which the British and Indian troops displayed throughout. There was no question of disloyalty in the Indian Army when the call of duty came.

The reader may decide for himself where the responsibility for the deaths of the gallant soldiers who perished in this campaign ultimately lay.

VIII

" NON-CO-OPERATION WITH A SATANIC GOVERNMENT "

" **India has had bitter experience of the fruits of . . . the *Sataygraha* cult, and the Governor General in Council still hopes that with that lamentable warning before her eyes, India will reject the much greater peril of non-co-operation. Its principal exponents have frankly avowed that their object is to destroy the present Government. . . . The full consummation of their hopes would leave India defenceless against foreign aggression and internal chaos."—*Government of India Resolution, November,* 1920.**

THE events described in the previous chapter had for the time a sobering influence on the anti-British faction in India. Mr. Gandhi himself, when he saw the results of his " passive resistance " movement, confessed that he had committed a blunder of " Himalayan " dimensions; that he had miscalculated the chances of *Sataygraha* being understood by the masses. He accordingly exhorted the people to abandon violence, and he announced his intention of fasting for three days by way of penance.

Yet in the following year, in alliance with certain Mahomedan extremists, he inaugurated another sinister movement which developed into outrage and murder and led to the terrible massacre of Malabar.

The Khilafat movement had its origin in the post-war settlement with Turkey, which was regarded by many Moslems as constituting a blow at their religion, and the avowed object of its leaders was to restore the Sultan, the Khalif of Islam, to the status he enjoyed before the Great War. Under the direction of Mahomed Ali and his brother, Shaukat Ali, this movement ultimately became a public danger which was accentuated by the proceedings of Mr. Gandhi, who called upon Hindus to join in the agitation. The Khalifat movement and the agitation for the redress of the " Punjab wrongs "—in other words, the condign punishment of officers who had participated in suppressing the rebellion—were coalesced, and Mr. Gandhi and his associates called upon Hindus and Moslems alike to cease to co-operate with what the former stigmatised as a " Satanic " Government. This non-co-operation campaign aimed at the complete paralysis of administration. Its adherents urged their fellow-countrymen to withdraw their children from schools and colleges controlled or aided by Government, and to set up " national " schools and colleges in the various Provinces. Lawyers and litigants were to boycott the British Courts; the military and the civil classes were to refuse to offer themselves for service in Mesopotamia, and Indians were to abstain from standing for elections to the new Legislatures set up by the Government of India Act. With few exceptions, lawyers refused to give up their practice in the Courts. But no small injury was inflicted upon the young in some parts of the country by withdrawals from schools and colleges, a process which ended when it was seen that "National" institutions could not possibly afford the necessary facilities for education.

The common-sense of India revolted from the prospect opened out by Mr. Gandhi's programme. Men of standing and influence emphasised the menace which it involved. The Government of India issued an appeal to the people to abstain from participation in a movement which contained the seeds of anarchy, and showed the fatuity of the promise of its leaders, that if their gospel were generally accepted India would be self-governing within twelve months. Mr. Gandhi gave pledges of this kind on several occasions; indeed in October, 1921, he declared that if Swaraj were not obtained by December, he would either die of a broken heart or retire from public life.

The Government of India also pointed out in their notification already mentioned that the appeal made to the ignorant and illiterate was fraught with danger and had already led to one deplorable crime, and they emphasised that the activity of the leaders, who went about stirring up excitement among the masses by inflammatory speeches and by the reiteration of false statements, might at any moment result in a serious outbreak of disorder. Still, the Government trusted to enlightened public opinion to dissipate the danger that enveloped India, and intimated that they had consequently refrained "so far as is consistent with public safety from repressive action, for they consider that such action should only be employed in the last resort, when indeed failure to adopt it would be a criminal betrayal of the people."

While educated opinion as a whole responded to the Government's appeal, the campaign among the masses resulted in serious disorders accompanied by unspeakable atrocities, and in the end strong measures were necessary for the suppression of a movement which menaced the very foundations of civilised administration. It is true that the frantic efforts of the non-co-operators, backed up in some districts by threats and violence, failed to prevent candidates coming forward at the elections for the Legislatures. But appeals to the ignorant had their inevitable result, and the violence created by the non-co-operation movement in the years 1920, 1921 and 1922 spread to every Province in India. The criminal classes made the most of the opportunities presented to them; the "national volunteers," recruited in some areas from the scum of the populace, resorted to gross intimidation and terrorism. Government and Government's officers were openly defied; in Malabar, the Moplah rebellion led to the temporary collapse of the civil administration. Rioting became widespread; persistent efforts were made to seduce Indian soldiers and police from their allegiance. In the year 1921 it was necessary to call out the military on forty-seven occasions, and Sir William Vincent stated in the Legislative Assembly in January, 1922, that during the preceding three months military assistance had to be invoked no less than nineteen times. Rioting in jails occurred in several Provinces, and organised attempts to break out of prison led to the loss of many lives.

The exponents of "non-violent non-co-operation" spared neither the living nor the dead. In Delhi, "volunteers" sought to prevent the funeral of a loyal Mahomedan; in Bihar they exhumed the body of another Mahomedan, threw it upon the public road, and beat in the face with a brick.

One of the worst of the many outrages arising from non-co-operation was the massacre at Chauri Chaura, in the United Provinces, in February, 1922, of twenty-two Indian policemen by a frenzied mob headed by "national volunteers."

The rioters attacked the police station, murdered the inmates in the most brutal manner, and burned the bodies of their victims after soaking them in oil. They then proceeded to cut the telegraph wires and dismantle the railway, threatening the stationmaster and the local post-master with death if they sent any message to the authorities at Gorakhpur.

But the most terrible of all the fruits of the incitements against Government were seen in Malabar. The Moplahs of that region, a fanatical and ignorant Mahomedan race, inflamed by the wild speeches of Khilafat and non-co-operation agitators, rose in rebellion and committed unspeakable atrocities on their Hindu neighbours. Moved to indignation by these barbarities, Mrs. Besant, who visited the refugee camps in which thousands of homeless people found sanctuary, bitterly reproached Mr. Gandhi and his associates. "Mr. Gandhi," she wrote, "may talk as he pleases about non-co-operators accepting no responsibility. It is not what they accept; it is what facts demonstrate. . . . The slaughter of Malabar cries out his responsibility. Mr. Gandhi asks the Moderates to compel the Government to suspend hostilities, that is, to let loose the wolves to destroy what lives are left. The sympathy of the Moderates is not, I make bold to say, with the murderers, the looters, the ravishers, who have put into practice the teaching of paralysing the Government of the non-co-operators, who have made 'war on the Government in their own way'." Could not Mr. Gandhi, she asked, feel a little sympathy for thousands of women left with only rags, driven from home, for little children born of refugee mothers on the road or in the refugee camps? "The misery," she said, "is beyond description: girl wives, with eyes half-blind with weeping, distraught with terror; women who have seen their husbands hacked to pieces before their eyes, in the way 'Moplahs consider as religious' . . . men who have lost all, hopeless, crushed, desperate."

A manifesto was issued by Mr. Gandhi when the rebellion was at its worst, in which he wrote: "The forcible conversions (of Hindus) are terrible, but the Moplah bravery must command admiration. These Malabaris are not fighting for the love of it. They are fighting for what they consider is religion, and in a manner which they consider is religious." He, therefore, asked the Indian Liberals to compel the Government to suspend hostilities and allow the non-co-operators to persuade the Moplahs to surrender. He was addressing the Liberals and not the Government, he proceeded, "because the Government could not have taken an inhuman course of destruction without your moral support." The inhumanity of the Government which aroused Mr. Gandhi's indignation consisted of the military and police measures which they adopted to save the unhappy Hindus of Malabar from death and worse than death, and to bring the rebellion to an end.

Following on the Moplah rebellion came the riots which resulted from the frantic appeals addressed to the masses to boycott the Heir Apparent to the British Throne on his arrival in India, and to join in demonstrations against the Government. His Royal Highness the Prince of Wales landed in Bombay on November 17th, 1922, and was enthusiastically greeted by crowds of Indians who had come out to welcome him. But the disorderly elements of the population soon asserted themselves. They attacked the loyal men and women who had gone out to meet the Prince; they stoned tramcars; they burnt piles of foreign cloth; they looted shops, and they foully murdered unoffending Indians, Parsis and Europeans. The situation became so grave that the services of troops had to be invoked, and before the disturbances were suppressed 53 people were killed and some 400 more were treated at the hospitals. In Calcutta on the same day, to quote Sir William Vincent, "the riff-raff of the city, under the guise of volunteers, were abroad, terrorising and ill-using law-abiding folk, and there were numerous instances of molestations of Europeans and Indians." The Committee of the Bengal Chamber of Commerce, the most influential commercial body in India, addressed a strong representation to the Bengal Government, calling for firm action to put an end to the lawlessness which prevailed. The Committee maintained that the *hartal* in Calcutta was the result of wholesale intimidation of the working classes, who were waylaid and threatened with violence and the wrecking of their homes. The people were assured that the British Government had ceased to rule in India, and, according to the Committee, were rapidly losing, if they had not already lost, all confidence in the Government. There was no question of wishing to repress the national aspirations of the Indian people. It was merely a question of whether the citizens of Calcutta were to be protected, for a continuance of terrorism must result in tumult, riot and bloodshed.

Mr. Gandhi's action after the Bombay riots was characteristic of the man. He issued a wordy manifesto, in which he admitted that he was " more instrumental than any other in bringing into being the spirit of revolt," and he announced that he proposed henceforth to observe every Monday a 24 hours' fast until Swaraj was obtained. He also intimated that the dangerous project of inaugurating " mass civil disobedience " which he, in association with the Congress leaders had decided upon, could not be started unless a non-violent spirit were generated among the people. This campaign was to have been commenced in the Bardoli taluk of Bombay, which in 1928 was once more the scene of open opposition to the Government.

We have seen that at the outset of the non-co-operation movement in 1920 the Government of India, while emphasising that inflammatory appeals to the masses were fraught with danger, had announced their intention of refraining, as far as was consistent with public safety, from repressive action. The policy thus enunciated came in for severe criticism during the ensuing disturbances. On November 26, 1921, however, Lord Reading announced at Delhi that all necessary steps would be taken to ensure that every man might carry on his lawful pursuits in his own way. This announcement was received with relief, though even now politicians who claimed to be Moderates protested against the " repressive " measures that had to be adopted in order to protect their own countrymen from terrorism and crime. Arrests of leading non-co-operators were effected under the Criminal Law Amendment Act, and Local Governments were notified that for the purpose of dealing with inflammatory speeches the application of the Seditious Meetings Act to any district in which it was considered necessary would be authorised. These Governments were also informed that the appropriate provisions of the Criminal Law Amendment Act should be utilised to combat the illegal proceedings of "volunteer" associations, which were threatening the peace of India.

The vigorous measures taken against the Congress and Khilafat volunteers, and the sentences of imprisonment passed on many political extremists had a beneficial effect. But lawlessness still prevailed in many districts, and the "repressive" action of Government was strongly condemned in the Legislatures. Mr. Gandhi, having recovered from his fit of temporary penitence, put forward in the Indian National Congress a programme of a more sinister character than non-co-operation. He proposed a great extension of the volunteer movement, for which all students of the age of 18 and over were to be recruited, and to organise civil disobedience to law. These proposals were formally adopted at Bardoli. Mr. Gandhi was armed with plenary powers to act. An attempt on the part of a number of Liberal politicians to mediate between the Government and the non-co-operators proved abortive, and in February, 1922, Mr. Gandhi presented an ultimatum to the Viceroy, in which he intimated that civil disobedience would be commenced in Bardoli unless all non-co-operating prisoners were released, and a policy of absolute non-interference with the "non-violent" activities of himself and his followers were inaugurated. The Government of India replied in uncompromising language. The alternatives that confronted the people of India, they declared, were such as no sophistry could obscure or disguise. The issue was no longer between this or that programme of political advance, but between lawlessness, on the one hand, and, on the other, the maintenance of those principles which lay at the root of all civilised government. Mass civil disobedience was fraught with such danger to the State that it must be met with sternness and severity.

In face of the stern warning of the Government of India, Mr. Gandhi proceeded to Bardoli to launch the "civil disobedience" campaign. At this juncture there occurred the massacre of policemen at Chauri Chaura, which has already been described. Mr. Gandhi thereupon decided that the "truthful and non-violent atmosphere which can alone justify mass civil disobedience" did not exist, and that his energies and those of his followers should be concentrated on "constructive" work. Before the end of the month he had executed another *volte face*. The Congress Committee, at a meeting at Delhi, while professing to accept the decision of its Working Committee at Bardoli in regard to the suspension of mass civil disobedience, passed resolutions in favour of "individual civil disobedience" whether of a defensive or aggressive character, and individual civil disobedience was defined in a manner which, as was truly remarked at the time, made the distinction between mass and individual action of little practical moment. Mr. Gandhi claimed that the Congress Committee had "substantially confirmed" the Bardoli resolutions, though it was obvious they had done nothing of the kind. The truth was that he had lost control of his former followers, and had aroused a spirit of lawlessness which he could not exorcise. On March 10th he was arrested on charges arising out of his subversive activities, and, as he frankly admitted that "to preach disaffection towards the existing system of government had become almost a passion with me" he was sentenced to simple imprisonment for six years. After two years of his sentence had expired Mr. Gandhi was released by the "Satanic" Government.

His Khilafatist coadjutors, Mahomed Ali and Shaukat Ali, had already been tried and sentenced for having at a conference held at Karachi called upon Mahomedan soldiers to desert. These men had been interned during the Great War for their active disloyalty, and when the Afghan War broke out, to cite Sir Malcolm Hailey, now Governor of the United Provinces, they "announced to their friends the astonishing proposition that it was unlawful to fight against the Amir, and that it was their duty to join in a *jehad* (holy war)." Another of their exploits was to preach the doctrine, in 1919, that the only course left for an Indian Mahomedan was to join in a *jehad* or migrate to a freer land. The dissemination of this doctrine resulted in an extraordinary movement which inflicted grave sufferings on thousands of devout but ignorant Moslems. In the summer of 1920 the preaching of the Extremists of the Khilafat party impelled many Mahomedans in Sind and in the North-West Frontier Province to the belief that it was their solemn duty to migrate from India, a land under the domination of unbelievers, to an Islamic country. This movement received stimulus from the dissemination of false reports of the occupation by the British of Mecca and Medina. "The *Hijrat*, or migration from one country to another, for religious reasons," wrote Dr. Rushbrook Williams at the time, "has played a considerable part in Moslem history; but its revival in the present year of grace presented to the student of politics a phenomenon at once remarkable and tragic." Tragic indeed was the fate of the emigrants. At the outset the migration appears to have received some encouragement from Afghanistan. But when the magnitude of the *Hijrat* was realised by the Afghan authorities, they decided to prohibit the entry of pilgrims into their country, which could not possibly provide for the thousands who were anxious to find refuge there. The sufferings of the emigrants were pitiable. The road from Peshawar to Kabul became a veritable Via Dolorosa. Many of the unhappy people died from sunstroke, exposure, exhaustion and thirst; worn-out women left their children by the roadside for any stranger to pick up. Some of the emigrants were sent to distant Turkestan; others appear to have tried to make their way to Turkey. Thousands turned back with sorrowful hearts to regain their homes. Their plight was the more deplorable in that, in the height of their pious fervour, they had sold their land and other belongings for almost nothing, and they were now destitute. Government did all that was possible to mitigate their lot, and was able to regain for many of them the property which they had abandoned in order to set out on their ill-fated pilgrimage.

Another striking instance of the effects of anti-Government agitation on ignorant people was provided in Assam. The Assam Valley was enjoying peace and tranquillity when Mr. Gandhi inaugurated his non-co-operation movement. But the virus was introduced there; the Swarajists advocated the withholding of supplies from the European residents, and a no-rent campaign was organised. The agitators assured the cultivators that they need have no fear of Government action; no one would bid if their land and goods were put up to auction, so that they would retain their property and keep the money payable as revenue. They were, however, soon disillusioned. They had failed to realise that the law empowered officials to remit the arrears due and to resume possession of the land, and the mere threat of resort to this procedure was sufficient to bring the campaign to an end.

Mr. B. C. Allen, late Commissioner of the Assam Valley Division, in an interesting account of the movement, states that the sudden change in the demeanour of the people from friendliness with to hostility against the officials was found in the misrepresentations of the non-co-operators. The people had been told that Gandhi was a god; that when this god came to reign over them land revenue would be reduced to one-fourth of the present demand; that forest dues and forest restrictions would be abolished, and "in ears which would receive the news with pleasure, it was whispered that opium could once more be grown and spirits distilled without fear of an Excise Department." When the people resumed their old friendly relations with the officials they admitted their folly. "Sahib," said the inhabitants of a village to Mr. Allen, "the *babu log* told us that Gandhi was Raja, and we believed them. Now that we know once more that you are Raja, of course we shall obey you."

A campaign of mendacity among the tea garden labourers caused great misery to the coolies. Thousands of them sold all that they had acquired by their industry for a mere song and set out to return to their far-off native villages which they had left in order to enjoy the many opportunities of material prosperity open to them in Assam.

The effects of the agitations which have been described were admirably epitomised by Sir Harcourt Butler, then Governor of the United Provinces, in 1921. After dwelling on the relief expressed by the people at the vigorous measures adopted by Government to restore order and vividly describing the outcome of the subversive movements which had been witnessed, he asked, "What have the Congress and Khilafat movements done? Satagrayha, which Mr. Gandhi himself pronounced to be a 'Himalayan blunder,' ended in disgrace. The attempt to boycott colleges and schools failed signally. It did not affect in this Province one per cent. of the students and scholars. The attempt to boycott the law courts was wholly unsuccessful. The appeal to surrender titles given by and offices held under Government fell on deaf ears. The efforts to seduce soldiers and policemen were almost in vain. But with each successive failure they have sown wider the seeds of racial hatred and the spirit of lawlessness. The results cry out against them and their works. Their hands are dripping with innocent blood; and the cries of ruined homes and ravished women have gone up to heaven."

I have described in some detail the outcome of the agitation set on foot in India in order to illustrate the grave dangers attendant upon the preachings of subversive doctrines to the masses. The menace is still there. During the year 1928 riots, sabotage, assaults on unoffending people and the derailment of passenger trains, resulting in heavy loss of life, have been the outcome of inflammatory harangues addressed to the participants in railway and industrial strikes. The speeches of Extremist politicians indicate a determination to carry on anti-Government campaigns, and the active intervention of Communist agents, drawing inspiration and money from Moscow, affords a warning which neither the Government of India nor the law-abiding classes can afford to ignore. The activities of the apostles of non-co-operation and "civil disobedience" have inflicted serious injury and loss upon India, without achieving any beneficial result, and the danger of a recurrence of these evils, so far from being chimerical, is real and ever-present.

IX

MENDACITY AND ITS BITTER FRUITS

"The campaign of unscrupulous misrepresentation has now gone to such lengths that it is difficult to justify further tolerance."—*Government of Bengal Administration Report*, 1928.

In the earlier days of British administration Government in India was compelled to resort to active and often protracted and costly measures to suppress the organised bands of marauders who preyed upon the people. During the last twenty years the authorities have been hampered in the work of improving the lot of the masses by revolutionary conspiracies and lawless outbreaks which have inflicted serious injury on the country and resulted in the loss of thousands of Indian lives. The Extremist politicians whose teachings have been responsible for these evils profess a lofty patriotism; they attribute systematic malevolence to the Government, and when stern action is taken to protect their victims, who are almost invariably Indians, they declaim against the "repressive" measures of an "alien bureaucracy."

The root cause of practically every outbreak,

apart from communal disturbances arising from disputes between Mahomedans and Hindus, is found in the propagation of anti-British slanders, and the pouring forth of an incessant stream of abuse of the Government and its officers, British and Indian alike. The violence of anti-British newspapers is almost incredible; no mendacity is too grotesque to find publicity in their pages, no innuendo too base to be enshrined in their editorial columns.

The history of the revolutionary movement which originated in Bengal in the early years of the present century, and which in one form or another has subsisted ever since, furnishes appalling evidence of the consequences of this campaign of calumny and falsehood. Speaking in the Legislative Council, on February, 1910, Sir Herbert Risley, after reciting a list of the crimes committed by the conspirators, declared that these were the natural and necessary consequences of the teachings of certain journals. "They have," he said, "prepared the soil on which anarchy flourishes; they have sown the seed and are answerable for the crop. This is no mere general statement; the chain of causation is clear. Not only does the campaign of violence date from the change in the tone of the Press, but specific outbursts of incitement have been followed by specific outrages."

Eighteen years later, in July, 1928, the annual

administration report of the Government of Bengal stated that the Press campaign of unscrupulous misrepresentation had gone so far that it was difficult to justify its further tolerance. The Criminal Investigation Department was represented as taking an almost fiendish delight in the fabrication of false evidence to support unfounded charges, although no explanation of such an amazing perversion of duty was never offered by a Press which itself recognised no obligation whatever to justify or prove the most astounding and libellous allegations. There was no need, the Government of Bengal remarked, for any newspaper to justify its existence by the excellence or completeness of its news. The qualities that go to build up a reputation were unnecessary to secure a circulation. Unbounded excitement and unrestrained vituperation provided adequate mental sustenance for a public whose taste had been degraded by many years of wild sensationalism. Further: "The evil results of a campaign of persistent vilification on an ill-balanced community have already manifested themselves in ugly and ominous forms, and the reputation and prestige of the official classes and of Government have been seriously undermined by the unending repetition of falsehood."

The communal differences between Moslems and Hindus had given rise to violent writing on both sides. Fierce threats and impassioned appeals to their respective supporters to be "up and doing" were published by rival editors. A Mahomedan paper addressed its readers in these words: "You should always bear in mind that the sovereignty of the earth as well as of the heavens belongs to you alone." On the other side a Hindu journal declared: "The crescent of *Id* will naturally fade before the effulgence of the *Vedanta*, the perennial source of truth, and that day is about to come."

The results of these communal incitements are evident, and the Bengal Government were impelled to assert: "The rising tide of communal hatred surging from the Press threatens to engulf the faint signs of unity that have appeared in recent years, and to destroy the foundations on which a few earnest builders have worked with so much care and patience." In India, as the bitter experience of the past few years has shown, violent language is too often followed by physical encounters between Hindus and Moslems resulting in bloodshed and death.

Is it surprising that there is unrest in India when so many of its newspapers delight in fanning the flames of communal hatred and in grossly misrepresenting every action of Government? The evil is not confined to Bengal, it is found in every Province in the country. Innumerable instances of the recklessness, and worse, of the anti-British Press might be cited, but two cases will suffice to show the nature of the pabulum which is served out to Indian readers.

In August, 1927, the Chief Court of Oudh dismissed the appeals of twelve prisoners who had been convicted in what was known as the Kakori revolutionary conspiracy case. Three of these men had been sentenced to death, the remainder to various terms of imprisonment. The crimes of which the accused upon whom the death penalty was inflicted were found guilty had been accompanied in one instance by horrible barbarity, the victims being their own fellow countrymen. On Christmas Day, 1924, an armed gang had attacked the house of a well-to-do villager in the Pilhibit district of the United Provinces. They shot this man twice, but neither wound proved fatal. The villagers assembled and threw bricks at the dacoits, who fired a number of shots in return. Six of the villagers were wounded, and a plucky village wrestler, who challenged the raiders to "come down and fight the matter out as between man and man," was shot in the abdomen and killed instantaneously. Ultimately the gang decamped with Rs. 1.600 in cash and three to four thousand rupees' worth of ornaments.

In the following March a similar armed dacoity was committed in another village in the Pilhibit district. The victims on this occasion were a cultivator, named Toti, and his brother, together with their wives and children. The dacoits resorted to violence and to torture. One of them seized Toti's young son, placed the edge of a knife at his throat, and threatened to cut his throat if Toti did not disclose the whereabouts of his money and valuables. Toti himself was nearly throttled. The point of a knife was placed against each of his eyes, and he was threatened with blindness unless he gave up his property. He was not, however, blinded, but he received a cut under one eye. Finally, a cloth soaked with oil was placed between the man's legs and set alight. Notwithstanding this treatment, he disclosed very little, but the dacoits managed to secure property to the value of eight or nine thousand rupees. In the course of the affair two villagers were shot, one of whom died from his injuries. A third dacoity took place in a village in the Partabgarh district. The man whose house was raided was wounded in the arm, struck three times on the head with a hatchet, and robbed of property of the value of two thousand rupees. The dacoits used fire-arms freely, killing one villager and wounding four others.

The final exploit of the conspirators was the robbery of a railway train near Kakori, some eight miles from Lucknow. The train was brought to a standstill by a man who pulled the communication cord of the alarm signal, the guard was overpowered and threatened with death, and a heavy safe containing railway money was thrown out on to the permanent way. While some of the gang were engaged in breaking open the safe, others maintained a fusilade of shots on either side of the train, and the passengers were warned that anyone who got out would do so at the risk of his life. A Mahomedan lawyer who disregarded the warning was shot dead. The dacoits escaped with some Rs. 4.553 in cash.

In the judgment of the Oudh High Court in this case it was pointed out that one of the bad features revealed by the evidence as to the methods of the conspirators was the manner of recruitment of youths and the conversion of the recruit into the recruiter. It had been proved that boys of thirteen and fourteen were approached by men of mature age and incited to become revolutionaries. The judges declared that the conspiracy was of a very serious nature, having as two of its proved effects the deterioration and ruin of young and impressionable boys and the ill-treatment, robbery and murder of countrymen of the conspirators. Of one of the leaders who was sentenced to death the judges said: "The gravity of this man's offences does not consist so much in the fact that he was engaged in a conspiracy to subvert the British Government. That is bad enough, but that offence is of minor importance in comparison with the other offences that he is proved to have committed. He has shown himself to be a deliberate, callous murderer. He was ready to murder harmless fellow-citizens against whom he had no possible grudge for the sake of his own objects." These pronouncements were made by a Court consisting of a British and an Indian judge who had carefully weighed the evidence presented to them.

I have described this case, which had many features in common with dacoities committed by revolutionaries in Bengal, in order to illustrate the attitude of the Extremist Press towards the barbarities perpetrated by so-called political criminals in India. Immediately after the murderers had expiated their crimes on the scaffold, the leading Swarajist journal in Bengal, in an editorial article, wrote that, whatever the nature of the offences of the condemned men, "we confess we cannot read without a feeling of awe and admiration the parting messages that they delivered as they approached the gallows with steady step and heads erect to receive the extreme penalty of the law that was inflicted on them in the name of Justice.

"Misguided fanatics, silly firebrands, wild criminals—call them what you will, but even after the whole dictionary of abuses and vilifications has been exhausted, there remains the little fact that a handful of young men so keenly felt the humiliation of the existing political situation in the country that the sweets of life tasted bitter in their mouth, and that they left their hearth and home to prove to their countrymen that the way to freedom lay through the gallows. . . . These men have died, but has the cause of justice and humanity gained? Has the system of administration that is responsible for these tragic deaths grown stronger thereby? Has judicial violence succeeded in eradicating political violence? Have potential revolutionaries been crushed out of existence? Or is the talk of justice mere camouflage? and Law thereby made the handmaid of organised brute force? Are these humiliating deaths but a precursor of the inevitable trial of strength, 'a small part of the price we have to pay if we would have the freedom which is the birthright of man'?"

A Punjab paper wrote bewailing the "tragic news of the execution of the four youthful victims of the famous Kakori case." (The ages of the three men whose appeals have been referred to were 25, 28 and 36.) They rode to the gallows, the paper went on to say, in a manner worthy of the patriots they undoubtedly were. "It is the tragedy of the public life of our country," it continued, "that it has been established as a sort of convention to regard even the noblest among our public workers, merely on the strength of their conviction by a court of committing acts of violence, as villains of the worst type, who deserve no credit for their services to the country and no sympathy for their sufferings. . . . We offer our sincerest condolence to the members of all the bereaved families over their great loss, but we would urge them to find solace in the fact that their sorrow is shared by a vast majority of their countrymen."

In view of the wholesale corruption of youth which has been a prominent feature of the revolutionary movement and the cruel crimes perpetrated by the revolutionaries on helpless Indians, it is astonishing that newspapers which express such sentiments should find wide circulation. The evil is one of long standing. During the period when assassination and attacks on villages by armed gangs, composed largely of young men of respectable parentage, were rife in Bengal, the movement was nurtured and encouraged by revolutionary papers. The Sedition Committee, presided over by Mr. Justice Rowlatt, to which reference has been made in another chapter, were impressed by the open incitements which had appeared in journals of this type. After a bomb outrage which caused the death of two European ladies, an informer, who was among the men arrested on a charge of complicity in the crime, was murdered in a

Calcutta jail. A newspaper, which was openly sold, commenting on the murder wrote: "Kanai has killed Narendra. No more shall the wretch of an Indian who kisses the hands of his companions reckon himself safe from the avenging hand. The first of the Avenger's history shall write of Kanai, and from the moment he fired the fatal shot the spaces of his country's heaven have been ringing with the echo of the voice 'Beware of the traitor's fate.'"

Among the documents examined by the Committee was a letter from a schoolboy in Sylhet to the editor of a paper which subsequently came under the ban of the law. This lad wrote: "From your advertisements, articles and your bold writings, I understand that he alone who has the subversion of the Feringhi Government at heart should by all means read the *Jugantar*. I, a schoolboy, living in a hilly country, don't feel any oppression of the Feringhi, and I give way before people for want of information. I am, therefore, in need of *Jugantar*, for it acquaints us to a great extent with the desire of driving away the Feringhis and also makes us alive to our wrongs."

The Rowlatt Commission justly observed that when the influences of the boycott ferment were supplemented by the perusal of such newspapers the impressions on many a youthful mind must have resembled those exemplified by this boy's letter. The publication of misrepresentations and slanders is indeed poisoning the minds of many a young Indian to-day, for these youths seldom have any knowledge of the other side of the case.

The propagation of falsehood from the platform is bad enough, its spread by the Press is worse, for it is incessant. Day by day in India papers are published which seldom if ever discuss intelligently the great economic questions affecting the people at large; co-operative credit, the improvement of agriculture and kindred problems are ignored, while every action of Government or its officers is perverted and the sole object of the British is declared to be the "exploitation" and enslavement of Indians.

One of the results of this mendacious propaganda is that these doctrines now find expression both in England and in the United States. It is quite common at meetings held in London to discuss various aspects of Indian life to find young students interrupting speakers with whom they do not agree, delivering impassioned orations denouncing the administration of their country, and asserting that India is deprived by British bayonets of the freedom she is striving to attain. In Hyde Park orators of the same type hold forth on the infamies perpetrated in their country by the British, and repeat *ad nauseam* exploded fictions that have done duty for half a century or more. Propaganda of this kind has assumed widespread dimensions in the United States, where Indian students and others seek to persuade American audiences that India lies bleeding at the feet of her British oppressors. This campaign has, no doubt, some influence in creating a sentiment of hostility among Americans against Great Britain, a result which its authors desire to achieve. Eminent Americans have, however, expressed warm appreciation of the work of the British in India, and it may be pertinent here to cite the pronouncement on the subject of an American gentleman, who had had long personal experience of India and the Indians.

During the Great War a distinguished American journalist, Mr. De Witt Mackenzie, made an extensive tour of India as a special representative of the Press of his country, and subsequently published his experiences in a book entitled *The Awakening of India.* Among those whom he interviewed during his visit was Dr. J. C. R. Ewing, the well-known educationist, who for a number of years occupied the high position of Vice-Chancellor of the Punjab University. Dr. Ewing said he was a friend of the British and a friend of the Indian, and he had always tried to maintain an unbiassed attitude in the consideration of all questions pertaining to the two races.

"And so," he added, "when I tell you that the stories of oppression which are being published in America are false, I speak from an impartial standpoint. The British Government in India undoubtedly has its faults, but I know of no Government which is perfect, not even our beloved American Government. I believe, however, that British rule in India has been a good thing. I believe that, on the whole, affairs have been conducted unselfishly and with the idea of doing everything possible for the advancement of India. Neither in taxation nor in any other way is the British Government oppressing the people of India. As a matter of fact, India is the lightest taxed nation in the world to-day, and the administration of equal justice for all has been one of the features which always has marked British rule here, at least so far as I have observed in my long study of this country."

X

THE DEPRESSED CLASSES

" I think all fair-minded persons will have to admit that it is absolutely monstrous that a class of human beings with bodies similar to our own, with brains that can think and with hearts that can feel, should be perpetually condemned to a low life of utter wretchedness, servitude and mental degradation, and that permanent barriers should be placed in their way, so that it should be impossible for them ever to overcome them and improve their lot. This is deeply revolting to our sense of justice."—*The late* Mr. G. K. Gokhale.

The existence in India of many millions of human beings who are regarded by the higher castes of Hindus as " untouchables " constitutes a poignant and a pressing problem. It stands to the credit of Mr. Gandhi that he has strenuously endeavoured to bring home to his co-religionists the necessity of putting an end to this injustice, but, so far, his efforts and those of other Hindu reformers have not met with the success that is sought to be attained. Caste remains a strong and deep-rooted system, though its regulations have been of necessity relaxed in great industrial establishments, like the Tata Iron and Steel Works at Jamshedpur, where men of all castes and races work side by side. But the distinctions of pure and impure continue to be observed, and innumerable instances might be cited to show that the beliefs on which they are based constitute a living and an insistent force.

The difficulty of appreciating how far the movement for removing the disabilities under which the untouchables labour is progressing was illustrated during the investigations of the Simon Commission at Poona. A telegram was published in the London Press summarising the evidence given by the Chief Secretary of the Bombay Government, in the course of which he said that the social life in the villages had remained unchanged, but the position of the depressed classes in the cities was better. "Frankly," Sir John Simon was reported to have remarked, "my impression, too, during our last cold weather tour, was that there is a considerable distinction between the city and country districts in this respect."

Two days later *The Times* published the following telegram:

"*CASTE IN BOMBAY SCHOOLS*

"(From Our Correspondent)

"BOMBAY, *Oct.* 18.

"The action of the Bombay Municipal Corporation in resolving that no caste distinction should be made in the matter of the drinking-water arrangements in municipal schools was strongly censured yesterday at a largely attended public meeting. A resolution was passed by the meeting condemning the Corporation's action, and describing it as contrary to the teachings of the Hindu religion. Another protest was registered by the Stock Exchange, which closed yesterday, and, although the Stock Exchange is generally ready to close on the slightest excuse, its action may be regarded as typical of the widespread condemnation of the Municipality's decision."

The opposition thus shown in a great Indian city to the children of a large class of the community being allowed to share the water supply in public schools must seem amazing to persons possessing no acquaintance with India. The history of the outcastes, especially in Southern India is, in fact, almost incredible. Dr. Whitehead, late Bishop of Madras, recalls that for a thousand years the outcastes suffered under the yoke of slavery. Old deeds of sale in South India used to state : "You may sell or kill them." Legal slavery was abolished long ago by the British Government, but a member of the Indian Civil Service told me that in recent years in Madras when he interfered on behalf of a pariah who was being oppressed by a landlord, the landlord retorted, "But this man is my slave." The success of British missions in educating and raising the status of the depressed classes constitutes a noble and inspiring record and provides an eloquent reply to the charge that the West is steeped in selfish materialism.

The extent to which untouchability exists was discussed at some length by Mr. J. T. Marten, I.C.S., the Census Commissioner, in the first volume of his report on the census of 1921. Mr. Marten asked Provincial Superintendents to furnish an estimate based on census returns of the approximate strength of the castes who were usually included in the category of "depressed," and he arrived at the conclusion that 53 millions must be taken as a low and conservative estimate of the total, since it did not include the full strength of the castes and tribes concerned, or the tribal aboriginals more recently absorbed in Hinduism, many of whom are considered impure. The numbers of these depressed classes, all of whom are considered impure, could, he said, confidently be placed at something between 55 and 60 millions in India proper. The degree and nature of their impurity, he added, varied in different tracts, and was most conspicuous in Southern India. These figures have since been questioned, it being contended that the number of actual "untouchables," excluding aboriginals and hill tribes, is about 30 millions. The question of classification involved is an interesting one, but, even on the basis of the lower figures, the victims of "untouchability" form 12 per cent. of the population of British India.

In the previous census report an attempt was made to give the names and numbers of the "untouchable" castes in the Province of Bihar and Orissa, but great difficulty was experienced at arriving at any reliable conclusion. Twenty-two castes were, however, returned as "causing pollution by touch or within a certain distance," and these at the census included about 8,825,000 persons. Speaking generally, said the Census Commissioner of 1921, "it may be said that not less than one quarter of the population (of the Province) consists of 'untouchables.'"

The Madras Government has adopted systematic measures to mitigate, as far as is possible by official intervention, the treatment which the Panchamas of that Presidency receive at the hands of the higher castes. It was stated in a report by the Labour Commissioner of Madras, issued in 1920, that in no less than six districts of the Presidency more than one person in every five was theoretically not allowed to come within a distance of 64 feet of the higher castes without pollution. The purificatory ceremonies were, however, generally neglected except by the most orthodox, but in some parts, especially on the West Coast, the restrictions were still very strong. The public water supply was absolutely forbidden in nearly every village to castes which numbered one-sixth of the population of the Presidency. In theory, all Government offices were open to persons of every class and creed, but a rich and respectable gentleman who had recently returned from abroad told the Commissioner that he was made to go outside a certain public office when it was discovered that he was of low caste. Again, though in theory all schools financed by public money were open to all classes, there had been great difficulty in giving effect to this policy. Five years later an official report to the Madras Government described the measures taken to insist on children of the depressed classes being given access to schools under public management. In some areas the opposition had been overcome; in others no children of the class named were admitted. There were in the Presidency 12,617 schools under public management, and in 4,850 of these admission was freely granted to children of the depressed classes.

A distressing account was given in the report of the Labour Commissioner already mentioned of the conditions under which the Panchamas lived. Many of their hamlets were extremely congested and insanitary. Many of the untouchables were cut off from access to the main village or the road except by permission of the owners of the fields the Panchamas must traverse. To reach their water supply or their burial or burning ground they were often at the mercy of the landowners. In many districts the Panchama field labourer was so tied up by debt to his master (who took care that the debt should not be redeemed) that he was practically a serf.

Under the influence of education and human sympathy great advances have been made by many thousands of the depressed classes. Official and missionary testimony shows that these people are capable, when treated as ordinary human beings, of rising in the social and educational scale. In recent years there has been a great stirring of the dry bones, and the "untouchables" have given outward and visible proof of a determination not to submit indefinitely to the social indignities and economic oppression under which they have laboured. In South India there have been riots owing to the attempts of outcastes to use the public roads which run through the areas in which the caste people live.

An instance of the bitterness of the hostility displayed in the villages towards social reformers was provided recently by a criminal case which came before the High Court of Allahabad on appeal. The appellants were eight Brahmins, who had been sentenced to transportation for life for having killed another Brahmin who resided in their village. According to the evidence, the murdered man had caused great provocation to his neighbours by trying to uplift members of the depressed classes. He allowed some of them to fetch his water and to perform other offices for him, and when they complained to him that their offerings at the village temple were refused by the Brahmins, he advised them to build a temple of their own, and helped them by giving them bricks. These proceedings led to serious trouble, and it was alleged that the accused men went to the offending Brahmin's house and called him out on the pretext of trying to arrange a compromise. When he responded to their call he was beaten to death with *lathis*, the long and heavy staves so often seen in the hands of Indian peasants. In the court below the Sessions Judge found the accused guilty, but being unable to say who had dealt the fatal blow he refrained from passing sentence of death. The Allahabad High Court agreed in this decision and confirmed the sentences of transportation for life.

Another case bearing on this question was tried in the previous year. An Indian non-commissioned officer holding a rank equivalent to that of lance-corporal, found it necessary to correct two sepoys, who resented his action because he was of a lower caste, and translated their resentment into action by assaulting him. The lance-naik complained to his Indian superior, who refused to punish the sepoys, but advised the man to assault them in turn. This he did by killing both of them as they were lying asleep.

A hopeful sign is found in the organised movement of the depressed classes to obtain a hearing for their grievances. Their anxiety regarding their position under the new regime in India is becoming more and more vocal, and they have now a nominated representative of their own in the Legislative Assembly. When the Royal Commission on the Public Services, under the chairmanship of Lord Lee, visited Madras the leaders of the outcastes stated in their evidence that the improvement in their position as a community had been in the main due to the British Government and British officials, and they expressed the fear that if the British Services were reduced they would lose what they had gained. In a memorandum submitted to the Commission on their behalf the view was expressed that the Indianisation of the Services and the elimination of the British element from the Government should be proceeded with slowly and carefully; so long as there was caste in the country, so long would there be the necessity for the British character of the administration through the agency of the British people.

The evidence of the representatives of the depressed classes in Bengal proceeded on similar lines. They also presented a memorandum in which it was stated that more than 95 per cent. of the posts under Government in the Bengal Presidency were held by members of three castes, who numbered about 2¼ millions, or one twenty-third of the total population. " Indianisation," in these circumstances, it was contended, would merely mean the strengthening of the hands of the three castes.

It is evident that the grievances of the depressed classes are being fully ventilated in the course of the inquiry by the Simon Commission. Their representative in the Legislative Assembly, Rao Bahadur M. C. Rajah, has been assiduous in his efforts to secure an improvement in their lot. Mr. Rajah in the course of an interview on the present Commission declared that when the Commission presided over by Lord Lee was taking evidence in Madras the representatives of the depressed classes were subjected to a severe cross-examination by two of the Indian members, and that at one stage Lord Lee had to remind one of the cross-examiners that "the witness is not in the box."

"The worst treatment meted out to our countrymen in the Dominions," said Mr. Rajah, "fades into insignificance before the trials and troubles undergone by the depressed classes in the lands of the so-called higher castes in India. They are still denied the use of public wells and tanks, and at the same time stigmatised as unclean. They are still kept out of schools and colleges maintained from public funds, and at the same time despised as ignorant and illiterate; they are still shut out from temples, and yet branded as ungodly. The Reforms have not as yet touched the fringe of the miseries of the depressed classes."

The ultimate solution of this problem rests with the Hindus themselves; meanwhile it is easy to understand the anxiety of the people concerned regarding their position under any further political Reforms that may be instituted in India.

XI

INDIA'S GRAVEST PROBLEM

"Let the leaders and thoughtful men in each community, the Hindu among Hindus, and Moslem among the Moslems, throw themselves with ardour into a new form of communal work and into a nobler struggle, the fight for toleration. . . . Let them begin each in their own community to work untiringly towards this end; boldly to repudiate feelings of hatred and intolerance, actively to condemn and suppress acts of violence and aggression, earnestly to strive to exorcise suspicions and misapprehensions and so create a new atmosphere of trust."—LORD IRWIN, *Viceroy of India.*

THE late Sir Alexander Muddiman once remarked in the Legislative Assembly that no nation could give self-government to another; self-government must be developed from within. That truth has received full recognition from Indians of eminence. Of all the obstacles that lie in the way of India's political progress on Western lines none is more formidable than internal dissension. The ever-present differences between Mahomedan and Hindu have been accentuated by the Reforms. The Moslems of India constitute a powerful force, but in point of numbers they are overshadowed by the Hindus. It was, therefore, necessary under the Government of India Act to provide separate electorates for the Mahomedans, so that they might secure a larger share of representation in the Legislatures than otherwise would have been possible. They cling tenaciously to this system; their accredited representatives emphatically affirm that it is essential that it should remain in operation. That such a system is inconsistent with democratic government is obvious, but any serious attempt to modify it would meet with uncompromising hostility from 70 million people who cannot forget that until the British came their forbears dominated India. The Mahomedans, in fact, were given special representation with separate electorates in the Morley-Minto Reforms, and the authors of the Montagu-Chelmsford report, upon which the present Government of India Act is based, remarked with truth that any attempt to go back on those arrangements "would rouse a storm of bitter protest, and put a severe strain on the loyalty of a community which has behaved with conspicuous loyalty during a period of great difficulty, and which we know to be feeling no small anxiety for its own welfare under a system of popular government."

It has repeatedly been made apparent that the Indian Moslems will not accept a system under which they would be dominated by the majority community, and their anxiety for their position is far more pronounced to-day than it was ten years ago. Perhaps the most outspoken and exhaustive exposition of the Moslem standpoint was contained in the Presidential address of Sir Abdur Rahim, delivered at the session of the All-India Moslem League held at Aligarh in 1925. Sir Abdur Rahim pointed out that the Hindus and Mussulmans were not two religious sects like the Protestants and Roman Catholics, but formed two distinct communities or peoples. Their respective attitudes towards life, their distinctive culture, their traditions and history, no less than their religion, divided them so completely that the fact that they had lived in the same country for a thousand years had contributed hardly anything into their fusion as a nation. "A mighty spiritual spell," he continued, "separates the 230 millions of Hindus not only from the 70 millions of Indian Moslems but from the rest of humanity, while it divides the Hindus themselves internally into groups which know no social commerce with one another."

Sir Abdur Rahim denounced the action of the Hindu politicians who were prominent in the Suddhi, the Mahasabha and the Sangathan movements, the professed object of the first being to convert Mussalmans into Hindus, and that of the last to train the Hindus for self-defence, while the Mahasabha comprehended all Hindu activities. The Moslems, he asserted, regarded these movements as the most serious challenge to their religion which they ever had to meet, and as a grave menace to their political status.

The communal situation to-day is if anything worse than when Sir Abdur Rahim delivered this address. Riots between Mahomedans and Hindus calling for military intervention are of frequent occurrence. Speaking at the opening of the meeting of the combined Legislatures at Simla in August, 1927, Lord Irwin, in making an earnest appeal for the cultivation of a spirit of toleration, said that during the seventeen months that he had been in India the whole landscape had been overshadowed by the lowering clouds of communal tension, which had repeatedly discharged their thunderbolts, spreading far throughout the land their devastating havoc. In less than eighteen months, so far as figures were available, the toll taken by this bloody strife had been between 250 and 300 killed and over 2,500 injured. Again, a statement laid on the table of the Legislative Assembly showed that from September, 1927, to June 30, 1928, there had been 19 serious Hindu-Mahomedan riots, these disturbances affecting every Province, except Madras, In a riot in Bengal 15 persons were killed, in two other cases in the Punjab the death roll was 24. The tension which prevails is deplored by sober Mahomedans and Hindus alike, and many attempts have been made to put an end to this deadly strife. But the efforts of the peace-makers have hitherto been frustrated, and it is beyond question that the violent anti-British agitation carried on in India creates an atmosphere favourable to outbreaks of communal violence.

The allegation that British officials regard these unhappy differences with favour is as false as it is malignant, and finds no support from responsible men on either side. The district officer's many responsibilities include the preservation of the public peace, and over wide areas in India the approach of a religious festival adds to his anxieties. Precautionary measures have to be resorted to in order to prevent bloodshed, the troops have to be warned that their services may be needed, and if notwithstanding all that has been done to preserve order an outbreak of rioting should take place, the officials concerned will almost certainly be assailed on the ground that they have shown favour to the one side or the other. The position of the Indian official in these circumstances is less tolerable than that of his British colleagues. If he be a Hindu he will inevitably be accused of partiality towards his co-religionists; if he be a Mahomedan the same indictment will be laid at his door.

Since his assumption of office as Viceroy Lord Irwin has striven earnestly to induce the leaders of the two communities to co-operate in an attempt to cope with the evil; in fact, one of the first of the notable speeches he has made in India was on the subject of Hindu-Mahomedan antagonism, which he described as "the dominant issue in Indian life." The most superficial analysis of the policy of the progressive realisation of responsible government in India could lead to no other conclusion than that the British Government recognised from the outset that harmony between the two great communities was an essential condition of the attainment of their goal.

Apart from considerations of high policy, it is impossible for anyone who has a friendly feeling for India to contemplate without profound sympathy the distress inflicted upon law-abiding citizens by the constant outbreaks of communal rioting. "We cannot enjoy our home life happily, nor do our festivals bring any joy to us," said a Mahomedan member of the Legislative Assembly during a debate on these outbreaks, and he added pathetically: "On the occasion of almost every festival more misery and sorrow are caused in every home."

It is often asserted by Hindu politicians that conflict between the two communities can be traced to the system of communal electorates. That contention will not bear examination. It is true that communal violence has been more frequent and more ferocious since the introduction of the Reforms, but the reason for this development is mainly to be found in the keenness of the struggle for place and power arising from the new political conditions in India. The organised efforts of Hindus to convert members of the Moslem community has been met by counter-organisation on the part of the Mahomedans, and reckless politicians and writers on both sides have consistently exacerbated communal feeling. The Mahomedans, being a minority and less advanced in education, are naturally anxious for their future; the Hindus, being a majority, feel assured of the position they would occupy under a democratic regime.

A notable illustration of the hostility engendered by the belief of the minority communities that their claims to posts under Government are not adequately recognised was afforded by a heated debate in the Legislative Assembly during the Delhi session of 1928 on the financial vote for the Customs. A Mahomedan member asserted that even an enactment of the Assembly regarding the representation of minorities in the Services would not remove the grievance, "because there is a huge monopolistic interest pervading the whole land, and they will thwart it at every step." It was contended by this speaker and by others, including a representative of the Indian Christians, that the minorities were not receiving their full share in the Public Services, and the allegation was definitely made that the Government's directions to the Administrative

Departments in this matter had failed to remove Mahomedan grievances. Nawab Sir Sahibzada Abdul Qaiyum, an eminent Moslem, who represents the North-West Frontier Province, declared that the satisfactory settlement of this question would go a long way towards putting an end to communal riots. He did not believe, he said, that the majority of these riots arose from purely religious sentiments; the "struggle for existence" was at the bottom of the whole mischief. It was to the interest of Government, and of all concerned that a proper division of the "loaves and fishes" should take place as early as possible, so that communal troubles and friction should be lessened. Mr. N. M. Joshi, who represents Labour interests in the Assembly, agreed with Sir Abdul Qaiyum that the main cause of communal strife was "this fight for jobs," which led educated men to rouse the passions of the illiterate masses. The views of these two members were strongly controverted by a Hindu leader, and the atmosphere became so heated that it was a relief when by the tactful intervention of the President a debate which had emphasised the antagonism of the two great communities was brought to an end.

So long as this struggle continues, suspicion of Indian officials of Government will be rife, though they perform their duties with honesty and efficiency. In a debate in the Punjab Legislative

Council, Sir Mohamed Iqbal, the famous poet, who as a public man is noted for the moderation of his views, said that after the 1927 riots in Lahore the Moslems sent a deputation to the Deputy Commissioner to express their distrust of the Hindu investigators employed by the police, and that a deputation of Hindus had waited on that official to voice their distrust of the Moslem investigators. Sir Mohamed Iqbal himself had gone with the Moslem deputation, and he cited the Deputy Commissioner's reply: "Before the Reforms British officers available for such work numbered 120; now they are 68. You both want European officers, but we have not enough to satisfy your request."

The task of dealing with communal disturbances and their outcome is a thankless one for British officers, civil and military alike. But when troubles do occur the cry for British troops immediately arises, and on several occasions British soldiers have been publicly thanked by respectable citizens for their services. After the communal riots in Rawalpindi, indeed, the inhabitants implored the authorities not to withdraw British military protection, although the civil officials considered that the presence of the troops was no longer necessary.

Unhappily there are politicians and writers in India who appear to delight in prolonging the strife of Moslem and Hindu. A terrible example of the results of wanton mischief-making of this kind was provided in 1927 in the Punjab in connection with the publication of a notorious pamphlet defaming the Prophet of Islam. The publisher was charged before a magistrate under a section of the Indian Penal Code which renders it a serious offence to promote feelings of enmity or hatred between different classes of His Majesty's subjects, and sentenced to 18 months' rigorous imprisonment. The conviction was upheld by the Sessions Judge on appeal, but the sentence was reduced to imprisonment for six months. The case subsequently came before the High Court of the Punjab, when the Judge, who belonged to a Sikh family but was by religion a Christian, while strongly condemning the pamphlet reluctantly acquitted the accused on the ground that the section of the Penal Code under which the charge had been brought was intended to prevent present attacks on a particular community, but was not meant to stop polemics against dead religious leaders, however scurrilous such attacks might be. This decision created widespread fury among the Moslem community throughout India, and had it not been for the sagacious attitude of Sir Malcolm Hailey, then Governor of the Punjab, and the courageous action of the Moslem leaders of Lahore in restraining their community, the gravest consequences might have ensued. The Punjab Government, by sanctioning the prosecution of an Amritsar paper which had published an article against the Prophet, helped to soothe the outraged feelings of the Moslems. In this case the offending Hindus were sentenced to terms of imprisonment, and subsequently a Bill was passed by the Central Legislature penalizing attacks on religion. These incidents illustrate in a marked degree the evil that can be caused in India by reckless men animated by senseless hatred of the adherents of a religious faith other than their own.

In his address to the All-India Moslem League at Aligarh, which has already been discussed, Sir Abdur Rahim contended that it was sufficient and best for them all to recognise frankly that in existing circumstances the presence of the English people in India was justified by necessity. "At the same time," he said, "we must point out to those Englishmen who would assume the rôle of political prophets that nothing useful is achieved by laying down that they cannot conceive of a time when the English would cease to be administratively connected with India." Political prophecy is often a vain pursuit, and it may be that the difficulties which beset the path of India's progress will be removed within a briefer space of time than now seems possible. If that end should be achieved and an Indian Government established strong enough to rule the country with justice and sufficiently enlightened to respect the rights of all communities and all classes, I believe every Briton who knows India and its peoples would, with all sincerity, wish it God-speed.

XII

THE IRRESPONSIBILITY OF THE LEGISLATIVE ASSEMBLY

> " If you pass this Bill and modify it until it becomes a great Statute, I can say—we can say—as I should like to say with the authority of the House to the peoples of India, ' The future and the date upon which you will realize the future goal of self-government are with you. You are being given great responsibility to-day, and the opportunities of consultation and influence on other matters in which for the present we keep responsibility. You will find in Parliament every desire to help and to complete the task which this Bill attempts, if you devote yourselves to use with wisdom, with self-restraint, with respect for minorities, the great opportunities with which Parliament is entrusting you.' "—*The late* Mr. E. S. Montagu, *in moving the Second Reading of the Government of India Bill.*

The hostility shown to the Royal Commission appointed in 1927 to inquire into the Constitutional position in India, and the attempts of a section of politicians to secure the boycott of Sir John Simon and his colleagues, aroused widespread attention abroad, and, in England, many people who had hitherto taken little or no interest in Indian affairs began to realise that a situation of some gravity had arisen.

In order to appreciate the actual position and to gain an idea of the task committed to the Commission a knowledge of the events which led up to the appointment of that body is essential.

The Act which created a new Constitution for India was passed with unanimity by the House of Commons at the end of 1919. It may be assumed that the great majority of the members of the House were inspired by the hope that the Reforms would mean the commencement of a new and brighter era for India. That hope, unhappily, was doomed to disappointment. The new Legislative Assembly which the Act brought into being consists of 145 members, of whom 104 are elected. This body possesses extensive powers, including the voting of a large portion of the annual Budget. Expenditure on the Army and on the Foreign Department is, however, excluded from its purview. The other branch of the Central Legislature, the Council of State, comprises 60 members, of whom 34 are elected. The Council has the same powers in regard to legislation as are vested in the Lower Chamber, but the Legislative Assembly alone is competent to vote financial grants.

In the Provinces Legislative Councils were created, and the system known as diarchy was established, under which certain subjects known as transferred, are placed in the hands of Indian

Ministers, selected from members of the Provincial Councils, while others remain under the control of the Governor and his Executive Council. The most important of the transferred subjects are local self-government, co-operation, education, public health and agriculture.

The inauguration of the Reforms was welcomed by many public men in India. Other Indians, who doubted the wisdom of introducing Western methods of government into an Eastern country, regarded the changes with misgiving. The great majority of the people, concerned only with the prosaic but all-important task of earning their daily bread, "cared for none of these things."

Non-official Europeans in India were not enamoured of the Reforms. But once the Government of India Act had become law they loyally accepted the position, and declared through their elected representatives in the Legislature that they would co-operate with their Indian colleagues in endeavouring to ensure the successful working of the Constitution. The pledge thus given has been faithfully fulfilled.

The attitude of Parliament towards Indian Constitutional Reform was clearly defined in the Preamble to the Government of India Act. The Preamble read as follows :

"Whereas it is the declared policy of Parliament to provide for the increasing association of Indians in every branch of Indian administration, and for the gradual development of self-governing institutions, with a view to the progressive realization of responsible government in British India as an integral part of the Empire: And whereas progress in giving effect to this policy can only be achieved by successive stages, and it is expedient that substantial steps in this direction should now be taken:

"And whereas the time and manner of each advance can be determined only by Parliament, upon whom responsibility lies for the welfare and advancement of the Indian peoples: And whereas the action of Parliament in such matters must be guided by the co-operation received from those on whom new opportunities of service will be conferred, and by the extent to which it is found that confidence can be reposed in their sense of responsibility.

"And whereas concurrently with the gradual development of self-governing institutions in the Provinces of India it is expedient to give to those Provinces in provincial matters the largest measure of independence of the Government of India which is compatible with the due discharge by the latter of its own responsibilities."

There was no ambiguity here. The time and manner of any advance were to be determined by Parliament, and by Parliament alone, and the action of Parliament was to be guided by the co-operation received by those upon whom new opportunities had been conferred and by the extent to which confidence could be reposed in their sense of responsibility. A clause in the Act itself provided that, at the expiration of ten years after the passing of the Statute a Royal Commission should be appointed " for the purpose of inquiring into the working of the system of government, the growth of education, and the development of representative institutions in British India, and matters connected therewith, and the Commission shall report as to whether and to what extent it is desirable to establish the principle of responsible government, or to extend, modify, or restrict the degree of responsible government then existing therein, including the question whether the establishment of Second Chambers of the local legislatures is or is not desirable."

It was thus the intention of Parliament that a period of ten years should elapse before the question should be considered as to whether it was desirable that the powers conferred upon the Legislatures should be extended, modified or restricted.

In September, 1921, when the Reforms had been in full operation about nine months, further sweeping changes were, however, insistently demanded by the Legislative Assembly. These demands were strongly opposed by several Indian members, but there was no question as to the support they received from the majority of the speakers. It was contended that the Assembly had already proved its fitness to exercise far greater powers, and the examples of China and Persia were cited as instances of the ability of Asiatic countries to govern themselves. Sir William Vincent, speaking for the Government of India, asked whether after so short an experience of the working of the new Constitution it was reasonable to affirm that it would be safe to confer complete autonomy on India from a fixed date in the near future. Could it be said that the electorates were sufficiently educated to appreciate the responsibility conferred on them? Were members aware that out of approximately 250 millions of people residing in British India there were only one million registered as voters for the Assembly? And were they aware that out of that million only about 182,000 recorded their votes at the elections? Was that not an indication that the electorate had failed to realise its responsibilities or the great value of the franchise given to it?

It was admitted on behalf of the Government that, so far, the Indian Legislature had showed promise of success. But it was emphasised with equal frankness that the British Parliament was not likely to lend its ear for a moment to the proposals which had been put forward. Ultimately, by way of compromise, the following resolution was accepted by the Government of India: "This Assembly recommends to the Governor General in Council that he should convey to the Secretary of State for India the view of this Assembly that the progress made by India on the path of responsible government warrants a re-examination and revision of the Constitution at an earlier date than 1929."

I met the late Mr. E. S. Montagu when, as Secretary of State, he visited India to conduct the investigation which led to the passing of the Government of India Act. Mr. Montagu was confident; he was honestly convinced that he was about to confer a welcome and a lasting boon on India. I saw him again at the India Office in 1921, just after the news had been received in London that the Assembly had demanded further powers. Mr. Montagu made no attempt to conceal his chagrin and disappointment. "We have," he said with emphasis, "granted these people a brand new Constitution, and now, before the ink on it is dry, they are demanding another. I will be no party to any change unless it can be shown either that the machinery of the Constitution has proved unworkable or that those who are working it have given proof of their fitness for further responsibility. Neither of these conditions exists, and I may tell you that my position in this matter represents the considered decision of His Majesty's Government."

In the latter days of his life Mr. Montagu had no illusions about India. If he had lived longer he would have seen further proof of the irresponsibility of the Legislative Assembly which, with the best of intentions, he had helped to create. The years immediately following the inauguration of the Reforms were years of strife and bloodshed in India, and, unhappily, the members of the Assembly have too often adopted implacable hostility towards measures designed to enable Government and its officers to suppress revolutionary conspiracies and to protect law-abiding citizens.

During the lifetime of the first Legislative Assembly elected under the Reformed Constitution, a number of useful measures were passed. Distrust of Government and its policy, however, manifested itself from time to time, and in the last session a proposal to enhance the salt duty, in order to meet the financial exigencies of the moment, was rejected. This decision was of more than passing importance. In the previous year, owing to a Budget deficit, the enhancement had been proposed by the Finance Member. It was, however, thrown out by the Assembly, and that ended the matter for the time being. In 1923 another deficit had to be faced, and the Finance Member made an earnest appeal for support for the increase. He asked "for one last long and strong pull, all of us pulling together, in the confident assurance that, so doing, we shall quickly get the boat out of the vicious current which is threatening to drag India down to the rocks of insolvency." It was shown that the increase of the salt duty from one rupee four annas to two rupees eight annas per maund of 82 lbs. would involve an addition of no more than three halfpence per month to the household budget of a family of four, and would therefore cause no hardship even to the poor. But the Assembly were unmoved by argument and by appeal. The declaration that the price at which the next Government loan could be floated depended in their action proved of no avail, nor did the irrefutable figures as to the incidence of the tax cause the opposition to modify their attitude. The people "would die like flies" if the increase were made, urged one legislator; another warned the Government that they were sowing the seeds of sedition. In the Council of State the increase had been carried by a majority of 28 votes to 10, and Lord Reading used his powers of certification under the Government of India Act in order to make it operative.

In a statement justifying his action which was subsequently published, the Viceroy pointed out that while a mill labourer was shown to spend approximately 56 per cent. of his income on food, salt represented only two-fifths of one per cent. The economic arguments against the tax, therefore, appeared to rest on shadowy foundations. His Excellency also declared that the use of his special powers could only be justified, in the words of the Government of India Act, "when it is essential for the interests of British India." In the present case the interests of India only, and no other interests, had been present in his mind. Unbalanced Budgets seemed to him to involve dangers to the future of India, and he was convinced that his action would prove of ultimate benefit in the development of the Reforms and the advancement of the country.

But this statement did not appease the opposition. One leading journal asserted that in issuing it Lord Reading had added insult to injury; in other quarters it was contended that a severe blow had been aimed at the Reforms. The truth was that, while objecting to the proposals of the Government for balancing the Budget, the opposition had no suitable scheme of their own for meeting the deficit. On economic grounds the case for the increase of the tax was unassailable, but that fact did not serve to prevent the setting on foot of an agitation characterised by the wildest exaggerations, and the dissemination of the palpably absurd statement that the certification of the tax was a deliberate insult to the Legislative Assembly, although no attempt was made to challenge the figures showing the incidence of the duty. It is well that the facts relating to this tax—which was soon to be reduced by one half—should be appreciated, since the attempt is often made to persuade the uninitiated both in England and the United States that it imposed a cruel and crushing burden on the Indian masses.

In November, 1923, the elections for the second Legislative Assembly and the Provincial Councils afforded marked encouragement to the Swarajists, whose organisation was much superior to that of their opponents. The Swaraj party had boycotted the first Assembly, but on this occasion they succeeded in returning nearly half the elected members. In the electoral fights for the Provincial Councils they were less fortunate, though they secured a majority in the Central Provinces. In the Bengal Council they proved to be the strongest individual group, though they did not command a majority.

The Swarajists made their position clear. They issued a manifesto announcing that they proposed to present an ultimatum to Government demanding the right for the Indian people to control their own destiny. If this were refused, they would carry on a policy of uniform, continuous and consistent obstruction, with a view to make government through the Legislative Assembly and the Councils impossible.

The first session of the new Assembly was marked by a display of strong hostility to the

Government of India. After an animated debate, a resolution was adopted by a majority calling for a Round Table conference to prepare a scheme for the establishment of full responsible government. This was followed by the rejection without examination, of four of the principal financial demands put forward by the Finance Member, and later by the rejection of the Finance Bill itself. The next step was to refuse leave for the introduction of an amended Finance Bill "recommended" by the Viceroy, in pursuance of the provisions of the Government of India Act, as containing only proposals for raising the revenue essential for carrying on the Government. The policy thus pursued had no reference to the merits of the measures involved; the reason for the rejections put forward by the leader of the Swarajists was that the Reforms were a failure, and that India's wrongs were unredressed.

In a statement explaining the reasons which had led him to use his powers of certification in regard to the Finance Bill, Lord Reading pointed out that the demands which had been restored by his Government had been rejected by the Assembly without any examination of the expenditure on its merits, and for reasons extraneous to the Budget. It was to him a matter of regret that the Assembly, to whom important responsibilities were entrusted in voting expenditure to be incurred by Government and authorising the provision of the necessary funds to meet that expenditure, should have failed to consider these important matters on their merits.

It would be tedious to follow in detail the proceedings of the Assembly. But it is pertinent to recall that at the opening of the session of the Indian Legislature at Simla in August, 1925, Lord Reading, after again affirming his own sympathy and that of the Secretary of State with Indian aspirations, and the determination of all parties in England to adhere to the declarations embodied in the Government of India Act, went on to say that the time for an inquiry into the Constitution had not yet come. The inquiry contemplated by the Act, he said, would be a genuine and impartial one. Nothing would be prejudged. He reminded the members of the Legislature of the words of the Preamble to the Government of India Act: "And whereas the action of Parliament in such matters must be guided by the co-operation received from those on whom new opportunities of service will be conferred and by the extent to which it is found that confidence can be reposed in their sense of responsibility." Then came the momentous declaration: "If those are to be the principles to guide the Commission to its judgment, I cannot think, as a friend of India, that it should commence its inquiries immediately. If the judgment of the British Parliament were to be pronounced upon the present evidence, I fear that it could but result in disappointment."

In the earlier session of the same year the late Sir Alexander Muddiman, then Home Member of the Government of India, an eminent Civil Servant, whose ability, patience and good humour were of inestimable value in the Assembly, had spoken on similar lines. In the course of another prolonged debate on a demand for the appointment of a Royal Commission to inquire into the Reforms, Sir Alexander emphasised the fact that the Commission, when appointed, would not come merely to register decrees that had already been formulated. The position of the Home Member he compared to that of a watchman on a tower looking into the darkness. The King's messenger came with the call, "Watchman, what of the night?" The answer he (Sir Alexander) frequently had to give was, "The night is very dark." "How long," he asked, "am I to continue to give that answer? When will the people of India enable me to say, 'The dawn is breaking'?"

Three years later, in March, 1928, Sir Basil Blackett, in his final speech as Finance Member of the Government of India, epitomised his six years' experience of the Legislative Assembly in these words: "What has been happening in the course of this last session is particularly depressing to a man like myself who has been in the Assembly now going back to a date very near its commencement. During the whole of that time the principal interest of many of us, the interest really that was the driving power behind what we were doing, has been the desire to make the Legislative Assembly more and more into a Parliament. My difficulty to-day is that I feel that at every turn this Assembly is to all appearance trying to commit political suicide. Every opportunity that is given it of showing that it has a responsibility and can use it, it takes to prove that it can be irresponsible."

The wrecking of the Reserve Bank Bill, which embodied the recommendations of the Royal Commission on Indian Finance and Currency, was one of the achievements of the Assembly in the Delhi Session of 1928. The object of the Bill was to provide India with a modern and efficient banking and financial system, and it had been prepared after a long and exhaustive inquiry by the Commission, which included both British and Indian financiers and business men. The majority of the Assembly, however, were determined to introduce political issues into this purely financial matter. They insisted that "the duly elected representatives of the people," to quote one of their spokesmen, must have a say in the administration of the Bank, and as this demand obviously involved grave danger to India's finances, the Bill was abandoned.

Another measure wrecked in the same Session was the Bill for the creation of an Indian Navy, which had been introduced by the Government in pursuance of the policy embodied in the Government of India Act. It was insisted that the control of the Navy should be in the hands of the Assembly, a proposition which was in direct violation of the Constitution, and the measure was accordingly dropped. The Assembly also refused to pass the financial vote for the India Office, and it rejected the vote for the expenses of the Simon Commission by a large majority.

A resolution placing it on record that the Assembly would "have nothing to do with the Simon Commission at any stage or in any form" was, moreover, adopted by 68 votes to 62. The mover of the resolution, the late Lala Lajpat Rai, said he had no faith in the Government or in the people who appointed the Commission, or in the competency of the Commission. "If the British Government think that by their withdrawal we shall be warring with each other," he observed, "I shall welcome even that condition, because after all, after a few years of warring and quarrelling and even bloodshed, we shall be settling down and forming some kind of government which will be our own handiwork, and which we can improve later on."

Sir John Simon had gone to considerable lengths in order to meet the demands that

Indians should participate in the inquiry which he and his colleagues had undertaken. In February, 1928, he put forward a proposal involving the creation of "a joint free conference," consisting of the seven members of the Royal Commission and a corresponding number of representatives of the Indian Legislatures, over which he would preside. With this end in view, the Central Legislature, comprising the Legislative Assembly and the Council of State, was to select seven members, and each Provincial Council a like number, for the purposes of the investigation. The Indian side of the conference would consist, when Central subjects were being dealt with, of the seven members of the Central Legislature; while in a Province the Indian wing would consist primarily of the Provincial members. The British Commissioners, on their part, would present their report to His Majesty, and the report of the Indian Committee could either be forwarded by the Central Legislature to Parliament, or, if the Committee preferred it, it could be made an annexe to the British report.

The opposition in the Legislative Assembly rejected this overture with contumely, and made strenuous efforts to induce the Provincial Councils to join in the boycott. At first the boycott campaign met with some success in the Provinces, but ultimately every Provincial Council, with the solitary exception of that of the Central

Provinces, decided to co-operate with the Simon Commission. The Second Chamber of the Indian Legislature, the Council of State, had no hesitation in electing three representatives to the Central Committee which was to sit with the Commission, and the Viceroy, at Sir John Simon's request, invited several other legislators to join that body. Sir John Simon's action in making this request to Lord Irwin evoked a display of righteous indignation from the leaders of the boycott. Moved by what a ribald critic might describe as unctuous rectitude, they forthwith issued a manifesto expressing surprise at Sir John's persistence "in evading the weighty and representative opinion of the Assembly," and the hope that the Viceroy "would not agree to perpetrate on the Legislative Assembly a grave constitutional impropriety amounting to a slight on its dignity and representative character." This typical protest was followed up by the modest demand that the Viceroy should forthwith dissolve the Central Legislature so that the "sentiment of the country" might be expressed on the issue.

It will have been gathered that the most disconcerting feature of the history of the Legislative Assembly is found in the opposition to measures designed to preserve internal order and to thwart the activities of revolutionary conspirators. A serious drawback to the conviction by the Courts of persons implicated in what is euphemistically described as "political crime" is the terrorism practised by the revolutionaries, whose threats against witnesses have often culminated in murder. Every exceptional measure resorted to by Government to protect law-abiding Indians against these men is characterised as "repression"; the police are accused of fabricating charges against innocent persons, and the higher authorities indicted as enemies of India's liberties. The hollowness of these charges received notable proof during Mr. Ramsay MacDonald's tenure of office as Prime Minister. Confronted with an outbreak of revolutionary crime in Bengal, the Labour Ministry gave their assent to the Bengal Criminal Law Amendment Ordinance of 1924 which, among other things, empowered the Bengal Government to arrest and intern any person in regard to whom there was reasonable ground for believing that he had committed or was about to engage in crimes of violence, or had interfered or was about to interfere by threat or violence with the administration of justice. It also provided that where a person had been arrested under the Ordinance a full inquiry should be made into his case by two experienced judges. Lord Reading, in a statement published at the time, described the objects of the terrorist organisations against which the Ordinance was directed, detailed some of the crimes which had been committed or planned, and declared that the Ordinance would in no way touch the interests or liberties of any citizens so long as they did not connect themselves with violent criminal methods. The Ordinance continued in force for six months, when it was replaced by the Bengal Criminal Law Amendment Act.

The action of the Labour Government in this matter should have warned the fomenters of disorder in India, that, differ as British politicians might on many questions of policy, every responsible party in England realised the imperative necessity of preventing revolutionary crime in India, whenever it was proved that strong action was demanded.

But the majority in the Legislative Assembly were soon to prove that they, at all events, had not changed their attitude. In the Delhi Session of 1927 a demand was put forward in the Assembly by the Swarajist party that all the détenus under the Act should be immediately released or brought to trial. In vain did Sir Alexander Muddiman, fortified by facts of the gravest nature, declare that men who had previously been amnestied had again engaged in revolutionary crime; that the conspiracy, though checkmated, had not been killed, and that it was essential that the Government should retain the powers with which they had been armed.

The majority of the Assembly proved obdurate; they refused to believe that terrorism ot witnesses had been so extensively carried on that it was impossible to bring men accused of complicity in conspiracies to regular trial, and they had no belief in the good faith of the Government. The proposal for the release of the détenus was carried by a majority of 13 votes.

The terrible results of seditious conspiracies have been described in another chapter, and when the injury inflicted upon India by these movements is considered, it seems almost incredible than an Indian Legislature should seek to withhold from the Executive the powers needed to checkmate the activities of revolutionary criminals. A still more glaring example ot the recklessness of the Assembly was provided in the Simla Session of 1928. The widespread labour disputes of that time, which were causing great injury to employers and employed, had been accompanied by serious disturbances, involving loss of life, by acts of sabotage and by the derailing of railway trains. Many passengers had been killed and many others gravely injured, and a sense of insecurity had been created among the public. It was notorious that the strikers were encouraged by Red agitators to persist in an attitude of uncompromising hostility to their employers, and Moscow, seeing an opportunity of creating trouble in India, promptly supplied the leaders with funds. It had been proved in the Cawnpore conspiracy case in 1924 that the prisoners had been in communication with the Communist International, and directions had been sent to India by one M. N. Roy, an Indian revolutionary acting on behalf of that body, who advocated violence and the destruction of property, and promised that at the propitious moment resources and armed help would be forthcoming from the International. There has, indeed, never been any attempt on the part of the Moscow Reds to conceal their intention of bringing about the overthrowal of the Government in India and of inaugurating a regime of wholesale confiscation. In view of the situation which had arisen, the Government of India introduced a Bill in the session of the Legislative Assembly held at Simla in the autumn of 1928, providing for the removal from British India in certain cases of persons not being Indian British or subjects of Indian States. The justification for the Bill was the preservation of the public safety, which was menaced by the activities of European Communists who had been engaged in fomenting trouble. From the very outset the proposed legislation was bitterly opposed by the Swarajist party. Attempts were made to persuade the Assembly that an intercepted letter of Roy was "a pure and simple fabrication and a forgery, and a forgery with a purpose," and that the Bill was a lawless measure put forward by the "bureaucracy" in order to increase their power at the expense of India. A leading Swarajist declaimed that it was futile to attempt to throttle Communist doctrines, and that "in the history of civilisation one will notice that the prophets have always been persecuted; they have been put on the cross or had to flee for their lives from their persecutors."

The operations of the Bolsheviks in regard to India will be discussed in another chapter. It may be said that the Bill was ultimately rejected by the casting vote of the President of the Legislative Assembly, and thus came to an end. If the votes of the official nominated members had not been given in its favour it would have been lost by a large majority.

A matter of concern to British commercial interests is found in the hostility displayed in the Assembly towards any proposal which, in the opinion of the majority, might possibly be of advantage to British trade. This attitude is as unreasonable as it is unjust. The policy of the Government of India in recent years has certainly not favoured British merchants and manufacturers; Indian interests have been rightly placed first, though whether all the measures adopted, especially in the matter of protective tariffs, will prove beneficial to India in the long run is an open question.

Sir Walter Willson, who served for years in the Assembly as a representative of commerce, uttered a serious warning on this subject at the annual general meeting of the Associated Chambers of Commerce of India and Ceylon in December, 1927. "What," he asked, "are the dangers that we must defend ourselves against, that Government is unable or unwilling to protect us from? It is the policy of anti-European discrimination and expropriation which affords a rallying-ground—sometimes the only rallying-ground I might say—for all the divergent and conflicting parties of Indian politics. . . . The Nationalist enthusiasm of the Indian politician coincides with and is financed by your Indian competitors, who are endeavouring, by means of political pressure, to win what so far they have been unable to obtain in commercial competition." Six years' experience in the Assembly, he declared, had impressed him with the danger which faced British commerce in India, and he could not avoid the conviction that British commercial interests both in India and in England were not alive to what was taking place in the political arena.

This weighty pronouncement of a leading business man possessing long experience of the Legislative Assembly forms a suitable commentary on a statement contained in the report of the committee of the so-called "All Parties'

Conference" which in August, 1928, put forward a scheme for placing India on the basis of a self-governing Dominion. The Committee, which was presided over by Pandit Motilal Nehru, the leader of the Swarajists, disingenuously remarked that they did not see why men who had put great sums of money into the country should be nervous, since "it is inconceivable that there can be any discriminating legislation against any community doing lawful business in India."

The question under discussion has assumed prominence through the appearance in the Legislative Assembly of a Bill to reserve Indian coastal trade to Indian shipping. That measure was strongly opposed by Sir George Rainy, Commerce Member of the Government of India, as an attempt at racial discrimination, and vigorously supported by Pandit Motilal Nehru. In addressing the Associated Chambers of Commerce of India and Ceylon on the subject in December, 1928, the Viceroy, Lord Irwin, referred pointedly to the projected legislation. While sympathising with the desire that India should have a mercantile marine, he declared that he was not in favour of "speeding up Indian enterprise by the heroic—I might even say dangerous—methods advocated in this Bill." Lord Irwin suggested that India could be helped to realise its ambition without resort to methods of confiscation, and he hoped the solution would be found in co-operation between British and Indian industry and commerce.

I must confess that, after listening to a debate in the Legislative Assembly, I have often experienced a feeling of hopelessness for India's political future. A few hours spent in the Council of State gave rise to a more optimistic sentiment. The proceedings in the Second Chamber of the Legislature are conducted with sobriety; the members of the Council in most instances are men of position and weight; they have displayed courage and independence in the face of clamour and agitation and have exercised a profound influence for good in public life. It was inevitable that the Council of State should be a target for Extremist jeers and ridicule; that it should be described as a subservient appanage of the Government of India. There is no foundation whatever for the charges levelled against it by the Swarajists. The Council has a small majority of elected members; the remainder are appointed by nomination. At the inauguration of the Indian Legislature His Royal Highness the Duke of Connaught declared that the intention of Parliament was to create a true Senate, "a body of Elder Statesmen endowed with mature knowledge, experience of the world and consequent sobriety of judgment." In this aim Parliament was undoubtedly successful. The history of the Council has shown that India, so far from being bankrupt in statesmanship, possesses public men of high calibre animated by a sincere desire to advance the interests of their country and to make the best use of the opportunities afforded them by the Constitutional Reforms.

"The division lists of this Council," said Lord Reading in 1925, "furnish an abiding record that the nominated non-officials have not hesitated to vote against Government at the dictates of their reason or their conscience. On the other hand, they have not shrunk from shouldering the burden of temporary unpopularity which too often is incurred by those who, undisturbed by waves of passion and prejudice, have applied a calm and sober judgment, and have voted with Government when they were convinced that the higher interests of the country required it, when they were satisfied that these interests were being faithfully served by Government." In bidding farewell to the Council, Lord Reading affirmed that in times of special difficulty they had rendered a high service to their country by fulfilling to the best of their judgment the responsible rôle assigned to them by the Constitution. The Legislative Assembly itself includes among its members men of position and influence in their own districts who have displayed a sense of responsibility throughout their public careers. But unhappily these men have been overborne by the intransigent element, consisting in the main of lawyer politicians, who, possessing no administrative experience, clamour for the control of Indian affairs.

XIII

SELF-GOVERNMENT IN THE PROVINCES

> "It is the fashion among a section of India's politicians to gibe at what they describe as the fetish of efficiency. But administration touches the health, the education, the material prosperity, and the security of the people, and any serious deterioration that it may undergo must inevitably react on the welfare of the community at large."
> —*Anonymous Writer.*

THE danger to India involved in any proposal to increase the powers of the Legislative Assembly is emphasised by the attitude adopted by that body towards questions involving the preservation of internal peace. It is, indeed, widely recognised by thoughtful Indians that there is pressing need for a modification of a system which places the Executive Government at the mercy of a Legislature which is neither representative of the people nor animated by a sense of responsibility.

On the other hand, expressions of opinion have been forthcoming from various sources in favour of conferring "autonomy" on the Provinces. "Provincial autonomy" is a term which seems to find favour with many persons, who do not appear to appreciate its implications or to be familiar with the divagations of some of the Provincial Councils. Diarchy may be a clumsy device, but where it has been worked with goodwill considerable progress has been made. At the same time, it is doubtful whether a unitary system would have been productive of better results in Provinces where implacable hostility to Government has been a characteristic of the Legislative Councils.

A flood of light is thrown on this question and on the conduct of local self-governing bodies by the replies of the Provincial Governments to a letter addressed to them by the Government of India in 1927, asking for comprehensive reports on the working of the Constitution in recent conditions.

These reports indicate very clearly that the operation of the Reforms has varied materially in different Provinces. Both in Bengal and in the Central Provinces persistent obstruction to Government measures which, if it had been unchecked, must have paralysed the administration, rendered it necessary for the Governor not only to use his statutory powers to provide the funds required for carrying on the work of the Province, but to take over himself the subjects transferred by the Government of India Act to Ministers responsible to the Councils.

In the Punjab, Bombay, Madras and the United Provinces a different picture has been prescribed. The Government of the Punjab, replying to the enquiries of the Government of India, remarked that, though occasionally inspired by the idea of placating advanced public opinion, the Council had approached most questions in a spirit of moderation, tempered perhaps by a disposition towards criticism of Government measures. Political theories, they added, were as a rule a secondary consideration with a majority of Punjab representatives, whose chief concern lay in the problems of actual administration, and in the material development of their Province and districts. The Bombay Government, again, after remarking on the inability of the Indian Ministers to embark on large schemes of social or educational advance owing to financial difficulties, went on to state that the Legislative Council had a large record of useful legislation to its credit. Its influence on both sides of the administration had been constant and considerable, and its attitude on financial and general matters had on the whole not been unreasonable. The Madras Government provided testimony of a similar character. The one-time professed Swarajist policy of consistent and continuous obstruction, they said, had practically never been pursued in Madras, and, on the whole, the Madras Council had adapted itself well to the observance of Parliamentary decorum as to the assertion of Parliamentary rights. They emphasised, however, that until literacy was much wider spread and of a higher degree the Council would always be functioning above the head of the average voter.

From the United Provinces the reply was not unfavourable. Diarchy, the Government stated, had now functioned for seven years: the administration had been carried on without a break, and on the whole, peacefully; revenues had increased and more money had been spent upon developments in many directions. Ministers had acquired insight into public problems and experience of the difficulties of administration; and both in the Legislature and to some extent outside there had been a general quickening of interest in public matters. "But the gap between the Legislature and the people remains a profound one; and there is great cause for misgiving in the immense disparity between the work still to be done in qualifying the elector and the means which are so far in sight for doing it."

A depressing note was sounded by the Government of Bihar and Orissa, especially in regard to the Public Services. The Government declared that the ingrained determination of the Legislative Council not merely to control policy but to meddle in details of the executive administration was directly responsible for the feeling that Government officers were now required to serve two masters. The feeling of insecurity in the case of Services working directly under the department of Ministers was serious; their very existence depended upon the annual vote of the Council, and though in the last resort the Governor might interfere to save a Service, it was felt that neither the Governor nor the Minister might avail to save individual appointments. "There is solid ground for this fear in the past action of the Council, and the inevitable result is the tendency of members of these Services to regard individual members of the Council in some degree as masters of their fate, an attitude tending to demoralization and fatal to good work."

A sombre picture was painted of the deterioration in the position of the district officer. The opinion of the Bihar Government in regard to this matter is worthy of being cited at length: "The prophecy of Mr. Montagu that the district officer would find a worthy substitute for his past position in the training of men who can relieve him of much of his burden is far from realisation. The modern politicians, as elected to the District Boards and Municipalities, have no desire to be trained. They resent interference, and it is not possible for the district officer to continue making futile attempts to improve matters. This is where the Reforms touch him most nearly, and as he sees the structure built up by his predecessors in the District Boards and Municipalities travelling down the easy road to chaos and bankruptcy, he has strong doubts of the wisdom of the policy that the people should learn by their mistakes. The people who pay the cost of these mistakes have not the remotest conception that they have even had the opportunity of making mistakes, and pathetically reproach Government and its officers for allowing these things to be."

Those who imagine that the people of India are clamouring for further Constitutional changes might study with advantage the evidence of the Provincial Governments on the attitude of the rural voter towards the Legislatures. The educated classes in the great cities realise what representative government means, but they are a small minority; it is in the villages that the vast bulk of the population is found. The British Government has created legislatures without ascertaining whether the material for an electorate existed, and until an electorate which can appreciate the implications of representative government is forthcoming it will be impossible to carry out to the full the conditional pledges set out in the Preamble to the Government of India Act. Even in Madras, where educational progress has been marked, the Council, as we have been told, will always be functioning above the head of the average voter until literacy has become more widespread. The Government of Bengal state that, " as yet the electors do not take much interest in the elections," and further that, "though the electorate is not confined to the upper and middle classes, that part of the electorate which has some degree of consciousness of its powers is confined to those classes." The fact that the electorate takes so little notice of anything that passes in the Legislative Council is attributed by the Bengal Government to the illiteracy of a large portion of the voters. An enquiry held in 1926 elicited the "startling fact" that of the Mahomedan electorate 62 per cent. were illiterate, the percentage of illiterates in the case of the non-Mahomedan section being 41. A subsequent enquiry showed that of the persons actually voting at the elections for the third Council 50 per cent. of the Mahomedans and 33 per cent. of the non-Mahomedans were illiterate. Public opinion being negligible, the Bengal Government reported, members took practically no trouble to maintain relations with their constituents; in fact, "the recognition of responsibility to electors is absent."

A similar condition of affairs is reported from the United Provinces. "The rural voters know nothing of the proceedings in the Council"; and in most areas they are still amenable to the influence of their landlords. In general, moreover, "the bond between the small voter and his member is of the slightest." Among the educated classes in the towns the influence and importance of the Legislature are now better understood, but "the peasant still knows nothing of what goes on in the Council and is indifferent to most of the issues that are there debated."

In Bihar and Orissa "the work of the Council excites interest among the town people who read the newspapers and follow the course of politics, and in educated circles generally, but some 95 per cent. of the electors neither know nor desire to know what is going on." There are signs, however, that the circle is widening. At the election of 1926 it was still a common belief, as at the election of 1920, that voters were required to vote by Government order and the villagers were escorted by the village chaukidar (watchman) to the polling station. References to Mr. Gandhi still influenced the ignorant voter. Pamphlets and handbills exhorted electors to support particular candidates because the "Congress" directed it, "but the voters in many cases must have the vaguest idea of what the 'Congress' is or what it stands for." Nor is the evidence from the Central Provinces more encouraging. The members of the second Reformed Council returned in 1923 are said to have been, in a sense, real representatives of the electorates, since more than 57 per cent. of the voters polled in contested general constituencies. "But when the illiteracy and general inexperience of the average voter are taken into consideration, it is a matter of considerable doubt whether the majority had any clear idea of the probable effect of their vote or any definite knowledge of the policy of the Congress party and what it would lead to in the Council."

In reply to the question as to the extent to which the Council represented and reacted on public opinion, the Government of Burma stated that it was early yet to express definite views on this subject. No doubt the Council represented public opinion so far as it existed and was vocal, but not much interest was taken outside in the Council's proceedings. As for the extent to which relations had been maintained between the members and their constituencies, one member made an effort to address his constituents in a public meeting, but according to the newspaper reports, only the chairman and the reporters were present. Some of the members of the Council, however, had had private meetings with their leading supporters.

The evidence available emphatically proves that unless the electorate is extended the legislative bodies cannot be representative of all classes of the community. On the other hand, it is difficult to see how an extension of the electorate can be made until education is more widely diffused and people who have been accustomed to personal rule are able to realise the implications of a representative system. The proportion of Council electors to the whole population varies in different Provinces. In Madras it amounted in 1926 to 3·36 per cent., and 48 per cent. of the enrolled voters exercised the franchise. In Bombay the proportion was 4·03 per cent. for the Council and less than one per cent. for the Legislative Assembly. The percentage of electors who voted at the Council elections was 69·84 and at the Legislative Assembly elections it was 70·97. At the other end of the scale we have the Central Provinces, where the electorate equals no more than 1·1 per cent. of the population, and the number of male electors who recorded their votes in contested general constituencies at the elections of 1923 was equivalent to 57·4 per cent. of the names on the register. In Bihar and Orissa, which has a population of some 38 millions, the number of registered voters at the last elections was 375,000. In the constituencies which were contested 60 per cent. of the voters went to the poll.

The theory that misgovernment by representative institutions is preferable to efficiency under official supervision receives a rude shock when the record of local bodies is examined. In some areas progress has undoubtedly been made since official chairmen were replaced by non-officials; in others gross mismanagement, and worse, are rife. The Bombay Government reported that the success or failure of the local self-government bodies was more often than not dependent on the presence on the Councils of one man of outstanding influence. There was a growing interest in local bodies among the people, but that interest was apt to be warped by communal influences. During the three years covered by the report the growth of Brahmin and non-Brahmin strife in the Deccan and Karnatic districts had a serious effect on the administration of the local self-governing bodies, and resulted in a loss of efficiency owing to four cases: first, the tendency to make appointments on communal grounds, irrespective of the merits of the candidates; second, increase of corruption among the establishment due to slack supervision and reluctance to dismiss or prosecute defaulters who might be of the same class or creed as the majority of the councillors; three, hostility of the leaders of the same caste—due to personal rivalry; and four, efforts to secure special consideration for one section of the public only.

In the United Provinces the record of the big cities was stated to be "not unencouraging"; it indicated merits as well as defects, and the fact that the defects had been avoided or overcome in some municipalities was regarded as a hopeful example to others. Among the small municipalities there were a number which displayed public spirit and a desire to accept their responsibilities. Others were notorious for gross mismanagement and indifference to the public interest. The Government Resolution on the working of Municipal Boards for the year 1925-26 cites the case of the Bara Banki Board, of which "the Commissioner finds it impossible to say anything good." The staff was uncontrolled and discontented, sanitation was disgraceful. Ghaziabad was in almost as discreditable a state. The Board had not repaired the roads, it was reducing expenditure on education and its collections were bad. In Telhar "the late secretary and treasurer are being prosecuted for embezzlement, and there can be no doubt that there has been very scandalous mismanagement." The Hardoi Board was heading fast for bankruptcy; the Jhansi Board had failed to realise its position as guardian of the public interest; it frittered away its time and money on tennis courts, libraries and statues. In Ballia the Board would not realise that it was its duty to collect dues without respect to persons; the roads in the district were the worst roads the Commissioner had ever seen. This list the Government rightly described as depressing, and they added that the cases cited exhibited in their most extreme form defects which in some measure can be found in many other municipalities.

The Government of Bihar and Orissa also had a pessimistic story to place on record. Reports which they had received from various sources showed that there had been serious maladministration in the majority of the local bodies in the Province, both generally and in regard to education, and they emphasised that this deterioration had followed directly on action taken in the spirit of the Reforms. The relaxation of official control and the extension of the electorate had led to the return of men without experience of local administration, and intimidation was among the various methods used to secure the election of candidates. The Boards used their control over primary education for spreading their own political views; in many cases they appointed wholly unqualified persons to important posts; in medical matters they often preferred to take their own line rather than be guided by the knowledge of their expert advisers. "Meantime the misappropriation of public funds is generally regarded more as a subject for mirth or envy than reprobation, and it remains to be seen whether the successors of the existing Boards will be able to resist the temptation of the spoils of office."

In Bihar and Orissa, moreover, the control which the Congress party secured in local bodies enabled them to gain a dangerous hold on the primary schools and to push their political propaganda among the pupils. Several District Boards, indeed, directed that the schools should open daily with the singing of a hymn which Government had proscribed as seditious. These bodies adopted the characteristic method of appealing to the High Court for a reversal of the order proscribing the song, and were only brought to their senses by a stoppage of Government grants.

The Central Provinces Government hoped for the best. The state of accounts of local bodies had, generally speaking, deteriorated, the number of financial irregularities of municipal Committees rising from 3,433 in the year 1922-23 to 6,033 in 1924-25. The affairs of some of the local bodies were in a state of confusion. Allegations of unfair treatment of the employees were often heard, and the insecurity of their tenure and the lack of any legal provision for an appeal to an outside authority against the orders of local bodies had been the subject of frequent comment. The Government, however, consoled themselves with the belief that the instances of mismanagement and deterioration which they described are "naturally to be expected in the period of transition through which the local bodies are now passing" and "when things have adjusted themselves to the changed conditions, it is hoped that a higher sense of public responsibilities will begin to assert itself."

The outstanding example of municipal misgovernment in Bengal is provided by the Corporation of Calcutta. At the elections of 1924 the majority of the seats were captured by the Swarajist or Congress party, and "the well-drilled

Swarajist caucus administered municipal affairs from a purely political instead of a civic point of view." There were encroachments by the members on the powers of the Chief Executive Officer, which reduced his initiative and authority to a shadow, with the result that there was little check on the extravagance of the administration, while there was growing indiscipline among the staff. The most objectionable relaxations of the building rules were frequently permitted, "and the interests of the public subordinated to private or party claims." While arrears of unpaid taxes accumulated, the Executive was prevented from using coercive measures for their collection from persons of influence. The Corporation's balances were as a consequence seriously depleted, and "its borrowing capacity reduced, in spite of the warnings given by its responsible executive officers."

The varying degrees of success or failure which have attended the operation of the Reforms in the Provinces, proves the futility of treating as a homogeneous nation the peoples of a vast subcontinent with wide divergencies of race, language, creed and ideas. The authors of the Montagu-Chelmsford report made a special reference to these differences: "Thus from a bird's eye view," they wrote, "India is still a country 'marching in uneven stages, through all the centuries from the fifth to the twentieth.' There are tracts where it would be fantasy to dream of representative institutions. There are everywhere people so ignorant and so depressed as necessarily to lie outside the limits of any franchise which can at the outset be framed. Even within the limits to which the new Constitution can be applied, there are differences of conditions of which account must be taken in applying it."

The sturdy Punjab peasant has shown an appreciation of the opportunities opened to him which is a testimony to his good sense; in some of the other Provinces, opposition to Government and almost persistent obstruction in the Councils have bitterly disappointed the well-wishers of India. The facts are there and they must be faced.

XIV

THE INDIAN STATES

" With one accord the Rulers of the Native States rallied to fight for the Empire when war was declared. . . . They have shown that our quarrel is their quarrel, and they have both learned and taught the lesson of their own indissoluble connexion with the Empire, and their immense value as part of the polity of India."—*Montagu-Chelmsford Report.*

The magnificent response of the Indian Princes to the call of the Empire in the Great War appealed to the imagination of the West. But throughout the agitation for Swaraj the position occupied by the Indian States has to a large extent been ignored, although these States constitute the most stable element in modern India. The loyalty of the Princes to the British Throne is unchallenged and unchallengeable. In times of internal stress and danger their influence has been effectively exercised on the side of order and British rule, and they have whole-heartedly cast in their lot with the Empire when it has been faced with menace from without.

During the Mutiny of 1857 the co-operation of Indian rulers was a material factor in maintaining the British position, and in the Great War, as the authors of the Montagu-Chelmsford report have said, they showed that " our quarrel is their quarrel," and gave without stint their personal services and their resources to the cause we were upholding. The Imperial Service Troops maintained by the Indian States were placed at the disposal of His Majesty's Government, and did notable service on various fronts, and in addition some 116,000 recruits were provided from among the subjects of the leading States for the regular Indian Army. These totals, however, are incomplete, since figures from a number of the States were included in the Provincial returns. The official record of India's contribution during the world struggle, moreover, emphasised that despatches relating to the various Afghan wars, the Mutiny, and several Frontier expeditions had testified to the good service done by various contingents of State troops.

The population of the States to-day is 72 millions and they have an area of 700,000 square miles. The Maharaja of Patiala, addressing a London audience, questioned whether many of those to whom he was speaking realised that it would be possible to fly an aeroplane from the most northern border of territory ruled over by the Maharaja of Kashmir to Cape Comorin at the extreme south of India without traversing more than a few hundred miles of British territory.

The States, in fact, were so situated that the main arteries of communication, which were vital both for the safety and the well-being of the Indian continent, ran principally through State territory. These simple facts are sufficient to emphasise the importance of the States and their rulers, and abundant evidence exists to show that the Princes are determined that their position shall be fully recognised in any future Constitutional changes that may be made in India.

It is obvious, indeed, that the Reforms introduced in British India and the possibility of further changes being proposed have created apprehension among the Indian Princes. They contend that in seeking to satisfy the political claims advanced in British India, the British Government have failed to recognise the rights of the States and the nature of the Treaties entered into by them with the Paramount Power. Their attitude was clearly defined by the Maharaja of Patiala in a statement which he made in September, 1928. After declaring that the attachment of the Indian Princes to the Crown of England was unshakeable, and describing the attitude adopted towards the States by certain Indian politicians, His Highness went on to say: "The time has, therefore, come for us to make it clear that our political relations are with the British Crown, with whom our ancestors entered into engagements which we are proud to honour, and that we and our people will never submit to be governed by British India, over many parts of which our States in former times held sway."

In all there are some 700 Indian Princes and Chiefs, of whom about 230 may be said to exercise real authority. Of these 230, 108 are entitled to be called Sovereign, and while they have divested themselves in favour of the Crown of the control of foreign relations and the right of defence, the Crown has under the terms of treaties and agreement undertaken the obligation of protecting the States against foreign aggression and in the majority of cases against internal disorder. Now that the Princes are seeking to ensure the protection of their rights against an encroachment on the part of British India, they have produced a mass of evidence in support of their contention that their relationship with the Paramount Power precludes any interference with their States by the Government of India.

In the year after the Mutiny Queen Victoria's famous Proclamation declared that all treaties and engagements made with the Princes by or under the authority of the East India Company would be scrupulously maintained. This pledge has been repeated on several notable occasions. In 1911 the present King-Emperor at the Coronation Durbar at Delhi said: I rejoice to have this opportunity of renewing in my own person those assurances which have been given you by my revered Predecessors of the maintenance of your rights and privileges"; and in his message to the Princes and peoples of India at the outbreak of the Great War His Majesty stated: "Paramount regard to treaty, faith and pledges is the common heritage of England and India."

The Princes, however, maintain that in practice the Government of India have encroached on their treaty rights, and in 1918 they cited a number of these alleged infractions. The passing of the Government of India Act by Parliament in 1919 created a new situation. Under the Reformed Constitution the Indian Legislature has enacted measures which directly affect the Indian Princes and their subjects. The fixing of the exchange rate of the rupee, and the imposing of protective import duties, are cases in point, and the Princes who have no voice in the matter, contend that unless definite steps are taken for the protection of the States a legislative body representing a fraction of the population of British India will pass new measures by which the interests of 72 million people outside British India will be prejudiced.

There is force in the contention that when the Bill which subsequently became the Government of India Act was under consideration a definite policy in regard to the Indian States should have been announced. The famous declaration of

His Majesty's Government in 1917 clearly defined the future policy of Britain towards British India as "the increasing association of Indians in every branch of the administration and the gradual development of self-governing institutions with a view to the progressive realization of responsible government in India as an integral part of the British Empire." In this announcement no mention was made of the Indian States.

The authors of the Montagu-Chelmsford report on Indian Constitutional Reform, looking to the future, pictured to themselves an India presenting the external semblance of some form of federation. The Provinces would ultimately become self-governing units, held together by the Central Government, which would deal solely with matters of common concern to them all. But, the authors of the report went on to say, the matters common to the British Provinces were also to a great extent those in which the Indian States were interested—defence, tariffs, exchange, opium, salt, railways, and posts and telegraphs. "The gradual concentration of the Government of India upon such matters will, therefore," they added, "make it easier for the States, while retaining the autonomy which they cherish in internal matters, to enter into closer association with the Central Government if they wish to do so."

In the meantime, the report recommended the creation of the Chamber of Princes, which at all events has enabled the Indian rulers to consult with each other on matters of common interest. An important outcome of the creation of the Chamber is the Standing Committee of that body. It was this Committee which first formulated a request for an enquiry into the relationship between the Princes and the Paramount Power, with the result that a Committee of three, under the presidency of Sir Harcourt Butler, was appointed to enquire into the question and to suggest means by which the economic relations between the States and British India could be satisfactorily adjusted.

The case submitted on behalf of the States to Sir Harcourt Butler's Committee is intricate and voluminous, but it may be summarised briefly as follows:

The Princes maintain that their relations with the Crown are contractual in character, importing definite rights and duties on either side. They have, they say, surrendered their foreign relations and their right of making war and peace, in return for guarantees of external and internal security, and of perpetual respect for those portions of sovereignty which they have not surrendered. They point out that their obligations towards the Crown, and the Crown's duties towards them, have been defined in a series of written engagements, the sanctity of which has been admitted by successive Sovereigns of Great Britain. But they assert that, in everyday matters, the terms of these engagements are not observed by the Government of India, whose officers have for many years steadily encroached upon State rights. The Princes do not ascribe this process to bad faith: but explain it as arising from considerations of administrative convenience, the dominance of which over the sacred obligations of the Treaties has been caused by the Government of India gradually becoming the Government of *British* India. In consequence, they say, the Government of India always thinks of the convenience, of the advantage, of the development, of British India (for whose administration it is directly responsible) and does not consider the rights or interests of the States (in regard to which it is merely an agent for the enjoyment of rights and the discharge of obligations, contracted by the Crown).

The Princes further maintain that this subordination of State rights to British Indian interests has now become a habit: that this habit has hardened into a fixed cast of mind since British Indians rose to high office in the Government of India. They further explain that until about ten years ago the States, being isolated one from the other, were weak and could not protest jointly and effectively. Now that they are allowed to consult one another, they are endeavouring to convince Britain that the system is inequitable; and they have submitted to the Committee a great mass of evidence which they believe will demonstrate the need of a change. They are asking for three things (1) a share in settling any policy which affects the States as well as British India; (2) a voice in the conduct of the day-to-day business between themselves and the Crown's agents; (3) a system of impartial arbitration which will prevent the Government of India from settling disputes with the States to which the Government themselves are a party.

The Princes declare that they have no wish to be obstructive, and when once the existence of these rights, which their legal advisers claim for them, have been admitted, they say they will give, as they have always given, any concessions which may be necessary to ensure administrative convenience and the progress of India. But they call upon Britain to honour her word, as pledged in the Treaties, and not to permit obligations of honour to be set aside at the dictates of a new administrative policy.

These are the essential points of the case put forward; it is unquestionable that the issues involved are of the highest importance to the future of India.

On more than one occasion during the past few years the Extremist Indian politicians who are vociferous in their denunciations of the Government of India and their officers have adopted an attitude of hostility towards the rulers of the States. The Princes, however, have formally and definitely asserted that so far from being opposed to political progress in British India, they have every sympathy with the legitimate aspirations of that country. Their position in this matter was defined in the following resolutions passed in Bombay in March, 1928, which were adopted with unanimity:

"This meeting of rulers and representatives of State Governments (*a*) appreciates the wisdom of His Majesty's Government and of the Government of India in providing for an enquiry into the relations of the Indian States with the Paramount Power and with British India; (*b*) recognizes that the readjustment of these relations so as to secure the political future of one-fifth of the human race calls for the highest statesmanship on the part of His Majesty's Government and the people of British India, and on the part of the Indian States; (*c*) declares its resolve to devote to the moral and material progress of the subjects of the States the advantages resulting from the equitable adjustment of fiscal and economic issues; (*d*) affirms the intention of the Indian States to join with His Majesty's Government and with the Government and people of British India in working for a solution which shall secure protection for all interests and progress for all India; (*e*) reaffirms the abiding determination of the rulers of Indian States, as recorded in the last session of the Chamber of Princes, to ensure the rule of law in their States and to promote the welfare and good government of their subjects; (*f*) emphasises the dependence of the progress and prosperity of British India and the States alike upon the creation of constitutional means for the adjustment of relations between them; (*g*) reaffirms on the one hand the loyalty of the Indian States to the Crown and their attachment to the Empire, and on the other hand their sympathy with the aspirations of British India which they regard as legitimate."

XV

LABOUR CONDITIONS IN INDIA

> " The future of India may lie in its (Labour's) hands; its representatives ought to understand Indian problems; Labour members should be encouraged by every possible means to go to India and see the work of their countrymen for themselves. But they should go there with a little less self-confidence, a little less readiness to blame and to sneer."—LOVAT FRASER *in "India under Curzon and After."*

INDUSTRIAL labour in India constitutes a problem of no little complexity, due to a considerable extent to conditions peculiar to the country. The factory worker is usually a cultivator who has migrated from his native village in order to add to his income and returns there when it suits his convenience. The supply of labour is consequently intermittent, and, further, the Indian operative is far less efficient than his counterpart in Western countries. He also brings with him to the city the habits and customs of the village and falls an easy prey to the ubiquitous money-lender. While, therefore, the condition of Indian industrial labour, notably in Bombay, leaves much to be desired, it is entirely misleading to base rhetorical disquisitions on the evils of Indian industrialism on comparisons of wages paid in India with those ruling in countries where labour has attained a high degree of efficiency. There is a great amount of trustworthy evidence available to anyone desiring to inform himself on this question, but unfortunately certain politicians from England who have paid flying visits to India seem to have drawn their facts and their inspiration from sources which are neither well-informed nor trustworthy.

The most thoughtful of the reports written by British Trade Unionists who have visited India is that of Messrs. J. Hindle and M. Brothers, who went out as representatives of the United Textile Workers' Association. It is of especial interest that on his return to this country in 1927 Mr. Hindle stated: "Wherever we saw industry organised or managed by European firms, there we saw both native labour and housing conditions under better circumstances than in almost any district where labour is run by native employers." A similar statement was made twenty years ago by an eminent Indian public man, the late Dr. T. M. Nair. Dr. Nair, who had served on the Indian Factory Commission of 1907-8, at the close of his investigations declared that he must confess with shame that in his tour throughout India he found that his own countrymen as a class were more unsympathetic and hard employers of labour than the European manufacturers. Of course, he added, there were many notable exceptions. "But speaking generally, the labourers fared worse under Indian employers than under European. Even some of the most enlightened and educated Indian gentlemen with whom I discussed industrial questions had not a single word of sympathy with the labourer to express. They were all anxious to make up for lost time and to push on their industrial ventures and to accumulate wealth."

Messrs. Hindle and Brothers remarked on the fact that in Indian mills four times the number of operatives per loom or spindle are employed as are required in a Lancashire factory. They also stated that while the Indian textile mills had a sixty hours' working week of six days, it was doubtful if more than eight hours' work per day was obtained from the individual operative, time being allowed for prayers, bathing, smoking and other occupations.

Welfare work, the same writers pointed out, was no small charge on production costs, since a large proportion of public services provided by municipal and other similar bodies in Lancashire must be undertaken by the owners of cotton mills in India. The report under discussion also touched upon the unfortunate habit of the labouring classes to herd together in insanitary conditions. In Bombay the delegates noticed that, though the houses owned by the mills were better than those owned by private individuals, and the Government of Bombay had built tenements and let them at an uneconomic rent, the workers did not take advantage of the improved conditions. Notwithstanding dirt and discomfort, the poorer people preferred to live in privately-owned dwellings. They claimed that they had more freedom and independence in these dwellings, while in those owned by Government and mills they were not allowed to take in lodgers.

Messrs. Hindle and Brothers held no brief for the employers; on the contrary, they criticised certain features of Indian industrial life with severity. But they evidently endeavoured to present a balanced statement which should take account of all the factors in the problem. Their investigation, moreover, was confined to the textile industry, of which they had practical knowledge. The truth is that in India, as in other countries, there are good and bad employers, and general denunciations of the employing class as a whole must fail to carry conviction to unbiassed observers.

If trade unionists in England propose to help in the organisation of Indian industrial labour they will do well to avoid the methods resorted to by Mr. A. Purcell, M.P., and Mr. J. Hallsworth, who paid a visit of less than four months to India in the cold weather of 1927-28, as delegates of the British Trade Union Congress. In this brief period, they stated on their return, they travelled about 14,000 miles, or something like 120 miles a day; they addressed many meetings, they inspected textile mills, railway workshops, irrigation works, gold mines, oil fields, tea gardens, rubber plantations, peasants' villages, hospitals, and other centres of interest and activity. Their wanderings ranged from Dharwal in the far North to Coimbatore in the South, and from Bombay in the West to Dibrugarh in distant Assam. The enumeration of their activities may impress the uninitiated, but it will only cause wonder and amusement to those who have first-hand knowledge of the vastness of India, the diversity of its races, the characteristics of its peoples, and the conditions under which its many industries are carried on. Neither of the delegates apparently was acquainted with any Indian vernacular, so that their speeches to workmen must have been delivered through interpreters, and obviously the visitors could not question the labourers direct.

These serious drawbacks did not deter Mr. Purcell and his colleague from publishing dogmatic dissertations on Indian affairs. If they had gone to India in their private capacity their statements might be ignored, but their investigations were conducted at the instance of an important and influential body, the Trades Union Congress, and their report was published by the Council of that body and sold from its offices to the public. It is here that the mischief lies.

The delegates asserted that "as far as we can judge, it would appear to be the definite policy of the employing class in India to stabilise poverty on a permanent basis." They also wrote: "Our general conclusion on welfare work, as at present carried on in India, is that it is a delusion and a snare." They devoted a whole chapter to the tea industry and made fantastic statements regarding conditions in Assam, which the Indian Tea Association (London) vainly called upon the Trades Union Congress General Council to substantiate or to withdraw. The Council sought refuge in the evasive assertion that they believed their delegates reported what they saw, and when they were confronted with the eulogistic references to the planting community by the Linlithgow Commission, they simply remarked that they had nothing to add to their previous correspondence.

It may fairly be assumed that the Council found themselves in an equivocal position when faced with the facts. Although labour on the Assam tea estates is exceptionally well treated, the delegates had roundly declared that "the tea gardens of Assam are virtually slave plantations, and that in Assam tea the sweat, hunger and despair of a million Indians enter year by year." Again: "We refrain from narrating many other facts which were garnered, except the significant one that we witnessed a group of men, women and children working away together, while about five yards away was a planter's young assistant proudly hugging a whip. This we regarded as good proof of the 'contentment' prevailing among the tea garden population."

Now the tea industry in Assam owes its existence to British capital and British enterprise, and hundreds of thousands of Indian labourers of the very poorest class who migrated from their homes to the tea districts are to-day, as a result of their employment on the tea estates, prosperous cultivators of their own land. The area taken up in Assam by former tea garden coolies, the Tea Association pointed out, is over 318,000 acres, and an additional 233,000 acres is held by others who still work for a few days a month on tea estates in order to add to their incomes. In addition to their wages, which have steadily increased in recent years, the coolies are generally supplied with rice at prices below the market rates, and they have free firewood and free land for cultivation, as well as medical attendance. Most gardens allow maternity leave to the extent of three to six months on full or half-pay.

There are now no "punitive regulations" in operation, as was alleged by Mr. Purcell and his colleague. These gentlemen went further and asserted that the supposed regulations made it exceedingly difficult for the labourers to give up their work if they desired to do so, and that, in any case, the cost of return to their native villages was prohibitive. The fact is that if any labourer does not wish to continue his employment the tea gardens are bound to repatriate him at their own expense.

It is true that strikes have occurred among the labourers, notably within the past two years. But, in reviewing the reports of their officers on immigrant labour in 1926-27, the Government of Assam explicitly declared that the strikes which had occurred during the year arose from trivial causes; that in no case was there any serious grievance or evidence of settled ill-will between the men and their employers, and they concluded with the statement: "Tribute must again be paid to the tact and patience of the managers on the one side and the good sense of the labourers on the other which generally prevail on tea estates in this Province."

The Royal Commission on Agriculture effectively disposed of the allegation that labour in Assam is treated with barbarity. Its members were so impressed by the opportunities offered to workers there that they asserted that they were unable to find any justification for the prohibition in force in certain congested districts of the United Provinces against migration to Assam, and they recommended that it should be withdrawn "without delay." They also paid a high tribute to the services the planting community have rendered to India. Except in Bihar and Orissa, they said, plantations were usually situated in remote districts, and in addition to the economic benefits they conferred on the community generally by the introduction of valuable crops, their presence was in many ways of great service to the local population. "Communications," the Commission's report added, "are improved, local agricultural practice is favourably influenced by a good example, the wages paid to labour raise the general standard of living in the district, and in many cases educational and medical facilities are provided. Further, when, as is often the case, local labour is insufficient to meet requirements, plantations play a part in relieving congestion in distant areas by the immigrant labour which they attract. Owing partly to their remote situation, and partly to the fact that Indian interests have not in the past been largely associated with the planting industry, the benefit which India owes to the planting community has not, we think, been adequately realised by the general public."

The tea interests were thus exonerated by a

Royal Commission from the charges levelled against them and praised for their services to the community. The suggestion that the whip is used on the labour force on Assam gardens was repudiated with indignation by the representatives of the interests affected, and not the slightest attempt was made by those responsible for the allegation to justify it by evidence. The Tea Association, London, in their protest wrote: "A planter would no more attempt to use a whip on any of his people than would a works' overseer in this country, and if anyone were unwise enough to try, his fate would be the same in either country."

Industrial labour in India, as has been shown, is often inefficient. It is also to a large extent unorganised. Enlightened employers would no doubt welcome any judicious measures to increase its efficiency and earning power, and it would be an advantage to them and to India generally if representative bodies of the men were organised which could place before the employing classes any grievances affecting their constituents. But the cause of trade unionism is not likely to be advanced by assertions that it is the policy of employers in India to "stabilise poverty on a permanent basis," and that welfare work as it is carried on is "a delusion and a snare." In India, as elsewhere, there are employers who have honestly sought to advance the welfare of their workers. The Buckingham and Carnatic Mills in Madras, for example, have for many years been regarded as model employers. These mills are under European control, and they inaugurated the movement for providing education for their employees. The Buckingham and Carnatic Mills and a number of other companies, both European and Indian, give free medicine and medical attendance to their labour force; some have crèches for children and pay maternity allowances to women. The Empress Mills in Nagpur, which are controlled by Messrs. Tata, are noted for the amenities they provide for their labour; while the British India Corporation of Cawnpore, frankly recognising, as they say, their responsibility for the thousands of people who co-operate in their activities, provide free of cost medical attendance, nurses and teachers. They have well-equipped dispensaries, as well as mill crèches and schools for children; night classes, recreation grounds and a home for widows. They have also established a provident and superannuation fund for their workers. At Jamshedpur, again, the industrial city created by the great Tata Iron and Steel Company, the management have provided many amenities in order to advance the material, the social and the educational well-being of the employees.

There is indeed abundant evidence to show that the welfare work carried on by many enlightened employers has proved of marked benefit to the people, and it is as unwise as it is unjust to attempt to discredit these activities.

Advocates of the improvement of labour conditions in India would do well to bear in mind that rhetorical appeals to the masses are likely to be misunderstood by the men to whom they are addressed. The riots and sabotage which have been the concomitants of recent strikes show how quickly labour disputes in India degenerate into violence. Foreign Communist influences have notoriously been at work striving to foment revolt, not with the object of improving the wages and general labour conditions of the men, but for the direct purpose of subverting the Government. The readiness displayed by Moscow to provide the strikers with funds is indeed eloquent of the intention of the Bolsheviks to create in India, if they can, a condition of misery and misrule akin to that suffered by Russia. The elevation of the status of Indian industrial labour is an object worthy of support, but the activities of Communist agitators, if unchecked, must inevitably lead to the degradation of the classes whose cause these men profess to serve.

It may be said with truth that the Government of India have a creditable record in regard to labour legislation. They have participated actively in the International Labour Organisation associated with the League of Nations; they have passed a Factories Act which limits the hours of labour to sixty per week, provides for a weekly holiday, and fixes the minimum age for the employment of children at twelve years. In addition, they have placed on the Statute Book a measure of Workmen's Compensation and a Trades Union Act, and have passed legislation for the settlement of labour disputes.

Indian Swarajists frequently cite the example of Japan when seeking to indict the Government of India. Interesting light was thrown on labour conditions in that country by the masterly report of the Indian Tariff Board, presided over by Mr. F. Noyce of the Indian Civil Service, which investigated the condition of the Indian cotton textile industry in 1927. It was shown that while in India the hours of adult labour were restricted to 60 hours per week, in Japan there was no restriction whatever. In India, juveniles under 16 might not be employed in a factory for more than six hours a day; in Japan juveniles under 15 might be employed up to 12 hours a day in cotton spinning mills when a single shift was worked and up to 11 hours when two shifts were worked. Again, in India the employment of women and children by night was entirely prohibited. In Japan, on the other hand, both women and children under 16 years might be employed at night until June 30th, 1929. The

Board, therefore, held that to the extent that labour conditions in Japan were in these respects inferior to those obtaining in India, there was unfair competition between the Japanese and Indian industries.

Everyone who is desirous of witnessing an improvement in the lot of the Indian industrial classes will watch with sympathetic interest the proceedings of the Royal Commission which has been appointed to "explore all aspects of the labour problem" in India. The difficulties to be surmounted are formidable, but the time is ripe for devoting serious consideration to the issues involved.

It is eminently desirable, as the late Lovat Fraser said in the words quoted at the head of this chapter, that Labour members of Parliament should visit India and see things for themselves. But no one, however gifted, can begin to understand Indian conditions without some knowledge of the past history of the country, of the obstacles which the British have overcome and of the social and religious customs of the people. The Indian problem is one of enormous complexity, and the visitor who is intent rather on condemnation of the work of his fellow-countrymen than on learning the truth, has no difficulty in finding mentors who will readily furnish him with materials for presenting on his return home a distorted picture of the India of to-day.

XVI

THE RED MENACE

"The existence of the Red menace to India is no longer disputed by any sane person. It began as far back as January, 1919, when large funds were remitted by the Bolsheviks through Helsingfors to India on the eve of the serious revolutionary agitation which in April broke out into open rebellion in the Punjab and Bombay. It has continued ever since with steady persistence, the propaganda being carried on either by Indian agents instructed in revolutionary methods in the Bolshevist institutions at Moscow, Samarkand and Tashkend, or by British or Russian Communist agents sent to India for the purpose."—Sir MICHAEL O'DWYER.

THE public speeches and writings of Russian leaders provide abundant evidence of the determination of the Red Communists to persist in their attempts to bring about a bloody revolution in India. "The East," said Zinoviev, "is the main reserve of a world revolution. The proletarian revolution is aiming first of all at English Imperialism." A pronouncement of the Commission on Eastern Questions, made at Moscow, was to the same effect. "The Indian proletarian mass must be utilised by us as a reserve and bulwark for the Comintern in Asia," the

Commission declared, and they reported that a scheme was to be worked out for establishing direct relations with the Indian masses. It would be possible to quote many other statements of this nature from the official organs of the Third International, and additional testimony of a similar character is furnished by revolutionary writings, intended for dissemination in India, which have been seized by the police and produced in the Courts.

The failure of the Communist International to secure "good results" in the earlier period of their campaign in India may be traced to two causes: the vigilance of the authorities and the ineptitude and disloyalty to their Russian paymasters of the agents employed by the International. But there has never been any attempt on the part of Moscow to conceal the fact that it aims at overthrowing the existing régime in India by violent means.

A complete exposure of the methods resorted to by the Communist International was made during the trial of the accused in what is known as the Cawnpore conspiracy cause. Four of the Indians found guilty by the Cawnpore Sessions Judge of being members of a revolutionary conspiracy unsuccessfully appealed to the High Court of Allahabad, and the judgment of that Court left no doubt whatever as to the aims of the conspiracy or as to the methods which were advocated in order to overthrow the Government.

The leading spirit in the movement against India is a man known as Manabendra Nath Roy, whose real name is Narendra Nath Bhattacharji. Roy, who before the War was a well-known revolutionary in Bengal, has had an extraordinary career. He has been engaged in plotting in Mexico, in the United States and in Berlin against British rule in India; he has trained Indian revolutionaries in Tashkend and other Russian centres, and he is now in the service of the Communist International. Roy consistently preaches the doctrine that India can never secure "freedom" except by violent means. "There are many," he wrote in one of his articles, "who proclaim themselves 'non-violent revolutionaries.' One could just as well speak of a 'vegetarian tiger.'"

In a pamphlet which came before the Allahabad High Court, Roy outlined the programme which he desired to have carried out in India. "Mass action," he said, "thus begun will develop into organised agrarian strikes, into food riots, the plunder of corn-stocks and assaults upon large estates, with the idea of confiscation. . . . Reactionary pacifism must be repudiated. What burst out spontaneously at Gorakhpur, Rai Barelli, Chauri Chaura, Malabar, Central India, and what is going on in the Punjab must be developed by every possible means. Peasant revolts should spread like wild-fire from one end of the country to the other."

The High Court found that the men were guilty; that, however wild their schemes might be, they had entered into a conspiracy with each other and with Roy. Violence and destruction of property were to be encouraged, conflicts were to be precipitated, and at the propitious moment resources and armed help were to come from "the Universal Revolutionary Party, that is, the Communist International."

The judgment in this case is of especial importance in view of the amazing speeches delivered in the Legislative Assembly in the autumn of 1928 against the Bill introduced by the Government of India to enable them to deport European Communist agents who were engaged in fomenting labour troubles. In presenting this measure the Government were animated by a desire to protect Indian lives and Indian property, for except in one or two isolated cases, it was Indians who had been the principal victims of the outrages which accompanied the strikes of 1928. Communist agents were prominent in inciting the strikers, and Communist money was remitted from Moscow to India to promote the designs of the Third International.

The most terrible of the acts of sabotage committed during this period was the derailment of trains, both in Madras and Bengal. An appalling disaster at Belur on the East Indian Railway near Calcutta was traced to the removal of a length of rail, which caused a crowded train to dash into a culvert and led to the deaths of 17 Indian passengers and a European engine driver. A Swarajist newspaper subsequently published a letter, purporting to have been written by an eye-witness, in which the infamous assertion was made that Europeans had brutally murdered Indian passengers who had been injured in the disaster.

It might have been thought that, in these circumstances, the Legislative Assembly would welcome a measure to enable the authorities to rid India of foreign Communist agents. So far from this being the case, the Bill was violently opposed, and, as has been stated in a previous chapter, was ultimately rejected. At the very outset the Swarajist leader in the Assembly sought to obtain the President's ruling that the Bill was *ultra vires*. This attempt having failed, a debate of four days' duration ensued which ended in the measure being referred to a Select Committee. Upon its return to the House the Bill again met with a hostile reception, and upon a final division being taken it was found that 61 votes had been recorded in its favour and 61 against it. The President thereupon gave his casting vote against the Bill, expressing the opinion that, unless the mover of such an extraordinary measure secured a clear majority, he could not expect the Chair to give a casting vote in favour of the motion. Such was the fate of the Public Safety (Removal from India) Bill which, in fact, would have been rejected by a large majority but for the votes of the official members of the Assembly.

In the course of the prolonged debates on the Public Safety Bill the most grotesque arguments were used against the Government. It was asserted that the Bolsheviks had no designs on India; they were, in fact, represented as worthy people who were animated by a laudable desire to improve the world. One legislator compared them to Cromwell and his Ironsides; another called the Assembly to witness that when certain Russian Communists were accused of committing crimes in China the Soviet Government at once disowned them. This latter gentleman proceeded to announce that if the Soviet Government or the Bolsheviks advocated murder, or advocated violence, with a view to overthrow organised government in India he would be the first to attack them. "That is just what they do," interjected Sir Hari Singh Gour. "I am sorry for the ignorance of my friend," was the retort of the orator.

The late Lala Lajpat Rai, in a vehement speech against the Bill, declared that what the

Government of India wanted was moral sanction for anything they might do thereafter "in order to involve members of this House and those who are not inside this House, but who advocate a better system of government of their country, in trouble. It is in order to prosecute and punish them," he added, "that we are asked to pass this measure." The Bill, he asserted, was prepared in the interests of foreign capitalists and foreign exploiters. Another anti-Government speaker made the banal complaint that the Bill offended against "India's sense of hospitality."

The majority of the elected members were impervious to facts and to arguments. They had made up their minds, and the weighty speeches delivered by influential Indians on the other side failed to move them from their attitude of implacable hostility. Sir Abdul Qaiyum, spoke from his personal experience of Bolsheviks on the North-West Frontier, while Captain Hari Singh, a veteran soldier from the Punjab, pointed out that India was already suffering from the "bitter plague" of communal dissension, and warned the Assembly of the consequences of allowing another plague to be introduced.

A remarkable speech by Sir Victor Sassoon, who has important commercial interests both in India and in China, was especially pertinent to the issue. While Sir Victor was in China in 1926 members of the Nationalist Government in

Canton told him that the Chinese had sought Russian aid in reorganising their military forces because they could not secure the co-operation of any other country in this matter. In 1928, when he visited China again, Nationalist leaders informed him that after their rapid military successes against the North, they found that their Russian advisers were no longer willing to co-operate loyally with them, but insisted that China should develop not on Chinese Nationalist lines but on the internationalist lines of Soviet Russia. The Nationalist Government found that the part of China under their sway was riddled with Communist cells, and as argument was wasted on avowed Reds, the authorities sent soldiers not only to the towns but to the villages to execute every Chinese Communist whom they could find.

"If this Bill is thrown out," said Sir Victor Sassoon, "what will the world's opinion be? That the elected legislators of this country are so wrapt up with their petty political considerations that they are not only prepared to cut off their noses to spite their faces, but that they are prepared even to risk doing damage to their country, merely to enable them to use the slogan, 'We have defeated the Government once more.'"

The Government, as we have seen, were defeated, the majority of the Legislative Assembly having again given a crude yet significant demonstration of their want of responsibility.

The gravity of the Bolshevist menace had previously been emphasised in a debate in the Council of State on a Bill passed by the Legislative Assembly to repeal the special enactments empowering Government to deal with criminals whose activities could not be reached by the ordinary law. The then Home Secretary of the Government of India, Mr. J. Crerar, in offering strong opposition to the proposal, gave significant information regarding Communist activities. The Government, he said, had documentary proofs that attempts had been made and were still being made by the Communist elements in China to secure connection with India. He also reminded the Council that the Government had accepted international obligations to receive and be responsible for India's own undesirables—that was to say, persons whose activities were likely to be dangerous to the peace and security of India or of other countries. Mr. Crerar disclosed the fact that the German Government had applied to the Government of India to agree to the removal from Germany of certain well-known Indian Communist agents, on the ground that their activities were obnoxious and dangerous to the German State. The Government of India were under an obligation to receive these persons, and Mr. Crerar pertinently asked: "Are we to allow them to carry out in India activities which in Germany were found to be dangerous to the State, and will this House seriously propose to deprive Government of the means of dealing with persons of this type?"

The Council of State by an overwhelming majority rejected the Bill which had been light-heartedly passed by the Legislative Assembly.

While seeking to promote revolution within the borders of India, the Bolsheviks have systematically planned to effect an invasion through Afghanistan. Their movement Eastwards has been marked by massacre and by the overthrowal of the rulers of Mahomedan States in Central Asia. The tragedy of Bokhara, in particular, is familiar to those who have followed the history of Soviet rapine and intrigue. The policy pursued by the Bolsheviks in pursuance of their design to strike a blow at the heart of the British Empire through India was to encircle India on the north by the creation of a chain of Soviet States, ethnologically grouped, and to permeate Afghanistan with their own doctrines.

Meanwhile, intensive propaganda has been carried on in Central Asia, and emissaries of Oriental nationalities have been trained in Tashkend to spread the virus of anti-British hatred in order to further Russian designs against India.

Although the gravity of the Red menace is apparent and its implications have repeatedly been emphasised by the highest military authorities in India, violent protests against the Government's modest expenditure on defence are incessantly forthcoming from leading members of the party which is demanding Home Rule. The Commander-in-Chief, Sir William Birdwood, in a striking speech in the Council of State in 1927, declared that it was necessary in view of the Bolshevist danger to keep a vigilant eye on the North-East Frontier as well as on the North-West border. "We know," he said, "what Bolshevist propaganda is doing not only in Afghanistan but in China. . . . If we were deliberately to reduce our Army in India, I have not the slightest hesitation in saying that India would suffer, and would suffer in a way from which she might never recover."

The anxiety of the Chinese Communists to spread the Red movement in the East found expression in an appeal addressed to the All-India Trade Union Congress, dated Shanghai, October 10, 1928. This document, signed by the Chairman and Secretary of the All-China Labour Federation, asserted that in spite of cruel repression mass uprisings of the peasants were spreading throughout China, and that large sections of Southern China were already governed by the Soviets, established and controlled by the local revolutionary workers and Red Army soldiers. It urged the necessity of common action by the proletariat of the world, and expressed regret that many of those connected with the Indian Trade Union Congress had joined hands with the "treacherous leaders" of the British Labour Party and the General Council of the British Trade Union Congress.

Another appeal to the Indian Trade Union Congress of equal significance was published simultaneously in a Communist paper. This appeal emanated from the Executive Bureau of the Red International of Labour Unions, warned Indian workers against moderate leaders and exhorted them to link up with the fighting Red International. It concluded flamboyantly in these words: "Long live the militant working-class of India! Long live independent India, liberated from Imperialism! Long live a single class International, embracing the Unions of all countries, races and Continents!"

XVII

WHAT OF THE FUTURE ?

" Military strength, material strength, we have in abundance. What we still want to acquire is moral strength—moral strength in guiding and controlling the people of India in the course on which time is launching them."—LORD MORLEY, *on proposed Indian Reforms* (1908).

WHO can predict what the future of India will be ? The economic potentialities of the country are almost unbounded, the material condition of the people is steadily improving, marked advance is being made in education, and if the rate of progress in agriculture witnessed during the past decade is maintained, the prosperity of the cultivators will be greatly enhanced in the next ten years.

But, as has been shown in the preceding chapters, the peace of India is almost incessantly disturbed by communal dissension, and there is, moreover, no Province which has not suffered from subversive movements set on foot by reckless men in the name of liberty.

If unity existed the problem would be a simple one. The races of India, however, differ as widely as do the races of Europe. Differences of language, differences of creed, differences of political ideals obtain, and demands advanced from time to time in the name of "the people of India" represent only sectional claims based on shadowy foundations. Whatever decisions the Simon Commission may arrive at, it can be asserted with confidence that they will be denounced by the Swarajists and their allies. No Constitutional change that would be acceptable to sober Indian opinion or to the British Parliament will find favour with politicians of the Extremist school. The Extremists include within their ranks some who profess their willingness to accept Dominion status as a stepping-stone to complete independence and others who assert that independence alone can satisfy their aspirations. Among the latter are men like Mr. Srinivasa Iyengar, deputy leader of the Congress party in the Legislative Assembly, who is reported to have said, in the course of a newspaper interview, "An Indian can fill his lungs only with the oxygen of Swaraj or independence, but cannot breathe for long the mephitic air of Dominion status."

The party which professes to seek separation from the British Empire is growing in numbers and in assertiveness. I say "professes," since it seems incredible that men who owe their material prosperity and what political prominence they may enjoy to British rule should be blind to the consequences that would follow the departure of the British from India. Almost without exception, the apostles of this movement belong to the lawyer class. No man of standing among the martial races is associated with it. The staunchest upholders of order and of sane and progressive government are drawn from the classes which, in the absence of foreign intervention, would rule India with a strong hand if the British withdrew.

That enlightened and patriotic nobleman the Maharajadhiraja of Burdwan declared in an address in London in 1928 that, taking the condition of India from the time of the Moguls as a guide to the future, the lesson briefly was this: "If India is tired of white rule, and if the British be tired of ruling India, then India must be prepared either to be ruled by the yellow races, or by those brown races whose religion is other than Hinduism, or by Soviet Russia"; and he added, "I may be called unpatriotic, or even a traitor by those who, in their idealism, want an independent India, which geographically and racially cannot, alas! so easily crystallize; but I take the British connection as the only solution of India's problems." These views coincide with the declaration of Sir Umar Hyat Khan, the distinguished Punjabi soldier, which have already been recorded.

The fatuity of the demand for independence, indeed, must be present to the minds of the majority of those who put it forward. They know full well that in times of commnual trouble the presence of British soldiers is a safeguard against the spread of rioting and disorder throughout India, and that the Army in India, composed of British and Indian troops under British supreme command, is a sure shield against invasion by land. The British Navy, towards the maintenance of which India contributes the nominal sum of £100,000 annually, provides security for her immense seaboard.

Indian troops proved their indomitable valour on many a stricken field in the World War. During the fierce agitations of recent years many insidious attempts have been made to seduce them from their allegiance. But the Indian soldier has remained true to his salt, and between the class from which he is drawn and the Extremist politician a great gulf is fixed. The constant attacks in the Legislative Assembly on expenditure on national defence has not escaped the notice of the Army, nor will the military class soon forget the insult offered them by Pandit Motilal Nehru, the Swarajist leader, who asserted in the Assembly that the money remitted to their families by the men of the Indian regiments in China was obtained by looting the Chinese.

The preaching of independence may, therefore, be taken as a move in the political game. It is carried on by members of a minority which in the past has lost nothing by vociferously putting forward extravagant demands. The Swarajists are astute politicians, and they have striven to create the impression among their followers that they are feared by the Government of India. In this way they have gained fictitious prestige in a country whose peoples, in the main, are deferential to authority. The man who has inspired the Government with fear, the credulous argue, must surely be a great personage.

Though the gibe, " a Government from which its friends have nothing to hope and its enemies nothing to fear " levelled against the Government of India is unjust, it is nevertheless true that Indians of position whose loyalty to their country is above reproach have commented with bitterness on what they describe as the excessive deference shown by the British authorities to Extremist politicians. These politicians, in their turn, almost believe themselves that they have terrorised Government; hence the formulation of fantastic claims and the delivery of violent attacks not only on the authorities in India but on everything associated with the British name.

It is fair to the eminent Civil Servants who were charged with the duty of representing Government in the Legislative Assembly to remember that with the introduction of the Reforms they were faced with a new and strange situation. In the old Imperial Legislative Council the Government of India could count on a permanent majority; in the new Assembly they were in a permanent minority. Beyond that, it had been impressed on the Indian Civil Service that its members must no longer consider themselves as the Government, and that it behoved them to fall in with the new order of things. In these considerations, no doubt, may largely be found the explanation of much that seemed inexplicable.

We have seen that, faced with the dangers inherent in the sinister non-co-operation movement, the Government of India decided to refrain from resorting to what in the jargon of Indian politics are known as "repressive measures." They realised the gravity of the menace; they publicly announced in November, 1920, that the full consummation of the hopes of the leaders of the revolt would leave India defenceless against foreign aggression and internal chaos. Still, they trusted to enlightened public opinion to dissipate the danger, and announced that they had consequently abstained as far as was possible consistent with public safety from repressive action, which they considered should only be employed in the last resort when failure to adopt it would be a criminal betrayal of the people. The authorities were animated by a sincere desire to place no obstacle in the way of the working of the newly inaugurated Reforms, and it may be assumed that their hesitation to resort to the stern measures which were ultimately found necessary was the motive which inspired their policy.

The terrible consequences of the non-co-operation movement have been described in an earlier chapter. Sober India stood firm in its abhorrence of the methods pursued by the apostles of that creed. But by violent and inflammatory speeches the non-co-operators caused an upheaval which threatened the very foundations of order, and it will be disastrous to India if the lesson then taught has not been assimilated. The rodomontade of the politicians who are calling for the expulsion of the British need cause no serious apprehension so long as there is full recognition of the fundamental truth that the duty of a Government is to govern. The Legislative Assembly has given ample proof that it cannot be trusted to co-operate with the authorities in times of difficulty or danger, and the highest interests of India demand that no tolerance shall be extended to the clamour of politicians who, masquerading as defenders of freedom, offer implacable opposition to the legislative or administrative action necessary to secure to their fellow-countrymen protection from intimidation and outrage. Widespread misconception is too often apparent in England and the United States regarding the relative importance of men and events in India. The Constitution drawn up at the "All Parties" conference held in Lucknow in 1928, for instance, was looked upon by many as a serious attempt to provide a solution for a difficult problem. In reality it was nothing of the kind. So far from being representative of all sections of the Indian people, the Conference consisted largely of Extremists who, in season and out of season, denounce the British and all their works, and of dissatisfied Liberal politicians who had been active in advocating the boycott of the Simon Commission. The trusted leaders of the Moslem community and the representatives of the depressed classes publicly expressed their disapproval of the decisions arrived at, while the Indian Princes condemned the scheme so far as it affected them and their States.

Politicians who had been prominent in the deliberations of the Conference described their action as a "generous gesture" to the British. The spirit in which the scheme was put forward by the Swarajists was illustrated by one of their leaders, a member of the Legislative Assembly, who said that the Socialist programme put forward by one of the other participants appealed strongly to him "for that way alone can mass movement be revived, and without the support of the masses you cannot bring the British

Government down on its knees. The responsibility for rejecting the All Parties' demands will be entirely England's. Do they want peace or war? It is for His Majesty's Government to answer this question. We have offered the olive branch. If they reject it they must be prepared for war."

A little later the Committee of the Indian Congress passed by a unanimous vote a resolution which, while purporting to accept the proposals adopted at Lucknow, definitely announced the Committee's adhesion to the decision of the Congress at Madras that "complete independence is the goal of the Indian people" and that "there can be no true freedom until the British connection is severed."

While the agitation for independence is condemned by responsible opinion in India, it none the less contains the germ of serious mischief. The illusory promises held out to the masses during the non-co-operation campaign created, as we have seen, a situation which caused grave anxiety to Government, and in the end inflicted serious injury on the people who had been duped by the fantastic prospects offered to them. Is India to witness a recurrence of the unrest, the disorder, the rioting, the crimes and the destruction of property which were the concomitants of that subversive movement? The reply to this question depends on those to whom the responsibility for the maintenance of the peace is entrusted. There are significant indications in the speeches of Swarajists that another attempt may be made to use the less instructed of their fellow-countrymen as pawns in the political game. The welfare of India therefore demands that a policy of drift shall be avoided, and that while consistent efforts shall be put forward to secure for Government the active support of enlightened opinion, no toleration shall be accorded to those who incite the masses to lawless action.

The discovery that a plot had been hatched to bomb a train conveying the members of the Simon Commission provides another proof of the poisonous influence of violent racial propaganda. Repression, even in its legitimate sense, is distasteful to the British mind. But duty stands first, and no one realised that more fully than that doughty Radical statesman, Lord Morley, who, nurtured in a school of liberal thought, did not flinch from applying the necessary remedies for violent diseases. An ardent upholder of the liberty of the Press, he gave his ready support to the Government of India of his day when they were faced with an orgy of outrage, which was largely the outcome of seditious writings. To the contention that these incendiary articles were mere froth, he retorted, "Yes, they are froth; but they are froth stained with bloodshed." And when he was assailed for having been responsible for a system of repression, he replied: "You would not have me see men try to set the prairie on fire without arresting the hand. You would not blame me when I saw men smoking their pipes near powder magazines. you would not blame me, you would not call me an arch-coercionist, if I said, 'Away with the men and away with the pipes.'"

The enemies of Indian progress are not found among the British, whether in England or in India. The attitude of Parliament and of the British Government towards India has been made clear on innumerable occasions, while the British commercial community in that country, through their representatives in the Legislatures, have honestly striven to ensure the smooth working of the Reformed Constitution. In the memorandum which it submitted to the Simon Commission, the European Association, which represents the British non-official community, defined the considerations governing the action of its Council, including: "The wisdom of assisting the political and economic development of the country in which we live, with due regard to the benefit and contentment of its various peoples"; and: "The loyal acceptance of the Reformed Constitution and the retention of the Preamble to the Government of India Act, 1919, as an indispensable test for determining the time for each advance towards responsible government."

The Council of the European Association emphatically repudiate the suggestion that the members of their community are antagonistic to Indian political aspirations; their attitude, as they define it, has been that of constructive criticism while reform proposals were under discussion and loyal co-operation when the Reformed Constitution became law. The members of the European Association, while seeking no special privileges for themselves, ask for definite safeguards for the maintenance of their legitimate rights, and the request is by no means uncalled for, considering the tendency of a certain school of Indian politicians to advocate discriminatory legislation against British commerce.

The benefits conferred upon India by British capital and British energy are visible on every hand. Railways have been built, great industries have been created, an enormous overseas' commerce has been established by the enterprise of the British, and at a time when capital was not forthcoming from indigenous sources for the country's development it was readily provided from Europe. A policy of discrimination would injure those at whom it was aimed, but it would be of far greater injury to India. Has the danger been fully realised by the interests directly concerned? Sir Walter Willson, whose pronouncement on the subject has been quoted in an earlier chapter, evidently thinks that it has not. Six years' experience of the Legislative Assembly, he said, had impressed him with the danger which faced British commerce in India, and he was unable to avoid the conviction that British commercial interests, both in India and in England, were not alive to what was taking place in the political arena. This matter involves wide considerations; it affects the industrial prosperity of Great Britain, and consequently the employment of British labour.

It is pertinent to recall here that the importance of safeguarding the legitimate interests of commerce was emphasised in the Montagu-Chelmsford report, upon which the Government of India Act was based. The authors of the report pointed out that it was the duty of British commerce in India to identify itself with the interests of India, to take part in political life, and, having demonstrated its value to India, to be content like other industries to rest on the new foundations of government in the wishes of the people. "No less," they proceeded, "is it the duty of Indian politicians to respect the expectations which have been implicitly held out; to remember how India has profited by commercial development which only British capital and enterprise achieved; to bethink themselves that though the capital invested in private enterprises was not borrowed under the assurance that the existing form of government would endure, yet the favourable terms in which money was obtained for India's development were undoubtedly affected by the fact of British rule; and to abstain from advocating differential treatment aimed not so much at promoting India's as at injuring British commerce.

"Finally," Mr. Montagu and Lord Chelmsford declared, "it is our duty to reserve to the Government the power to protect any industry from prejudiced attack or privileged competition. This obligation is imposed upon it, if not by history, at least by the duty of protecting capital, credit, and, indeed, property, without discrimination."

A hopeful sign for India's future is found in the participation of all political parties in England in the enquiry entrusted to the Simon Commission. The pledges contained in the Preamble to the Government of India Act are accepted by Conservatives, Liberals and Labourists alike. Mr. Ramsay MacDonald, moreover, promptly and emphatically repudiated the suggestion that if the boycott of the Commission proved successful, Labour would, if it came into power, appoint another and more pliable body to conduct the investigation. In a telegram despatched by him to Mr. Vernon Hartshorn, a member of the Commission, Mr. MacDonald said: "It is reported here that if your Commission were successfully obstructed, a Labour Government would appoint a new Commission on another and non-Parliamentary basis. As you know, the procedure now being followed has the full confidence of the Labour Party, and no change in the Commission would be made."

Again, in an article published in a Labour newspaper, Mr. MacDonald wrote: " India has reached a great turning-point. What is its future to be? Is it to emerge from its generations of tutelage with smooth grace, and carrying the goodwill and ardent hopes of a united British Parliament, or is it to create trouble both internal and external—is it to arouse the watch-dogs of reaction, and delay its own development and progress by engendering strife and enmity and strengthening within itself those elements of discord which are its greatest enemies?"

In consequence of the position they have taken up, the names of Mr. Ramsay MacDonald and his leading colleagues are now anathema to the Swarajists. The late Lala Lajpat Rai declared that Mr. MacDonald, Mr. Philip Snowden and Mr. J. H. Thomas had started a definite campaign against India's aspirations for political liberty, and that their Socialism was a thin disguise for Imperialistic and nationalistic designs against other people's freedom. " We in India," he said, " have ceased to take British Labour seriously.

We have found them out." Mr. Chaman Lall, a young gentleman who has associated himself with Indian trade unions, asserted that "all classes in India are aghast at the betrayal by the Labour Party," and he added, "MacDonald and Company have written a shameful chapter in the history of both nations." Pandit Motilal Nehru shares the indignation of his followers. His entry into the arena elicited the caustic admonition from Mr. T. Johnston, M.P., that he should not presume to hector and lecture the Labour Party.

It is apparent that Labour members of Parliament who have recently visited India are no longer impressed by the Swarajist pose as champions of the masses. The process of disillusion was illustrated in the debate in the House of Commons on the Appropriation Bill in August, 1928, when Mr. Purcell, whose activities have already been discussed, repudiated Mr. Saklatvala's theory that the Indian people were suffering from Imperialism. His own diagnosis was that they were afflicted by "stomach trouble," and he unequivocally expressed the opinion that Swaraj would bring them no relief. Mr. Purcell, who had attended debates in the Legislative Assembly, spoke contemptuously of the attitude of the Swarajist party there, and towards the close of his speech at Westminster he said: "I hope we shall not accept the idea which is accepted among some people, that the Swarajists and Indian Nationalists are the people for the Indian workpeople."

* * * * * *

The truth is being brought home to thoughtful men and women of all parties in England that no apology is needed for our presence in India. The work we have done there is a great work and it will endure. But the task is not yet ended; a vast field for high endeavour still lies before Britain in India. Courage and patience are the paramount need of those to whom the duty of guiding the destinies of the Indian people is entrusted; courage to uphold the true interests of India in the face of calumny and insidious clamour, and patience to bear with mistakes honestly made. The British connection has proved of inestimable value to a country which in the past has suffered grievously from rapine and oppression, and is still the prey of internal discord. Upon the maintenance of that association unimpaired the political progress and economic prosperity of India unquestionably depend.

INDEX